NOBLE & WEBSTER

ΔΕΣΤΕ

DESTE Foundation for Contemporary Art

NOBLE &
WEBSTER

2000 WORDS

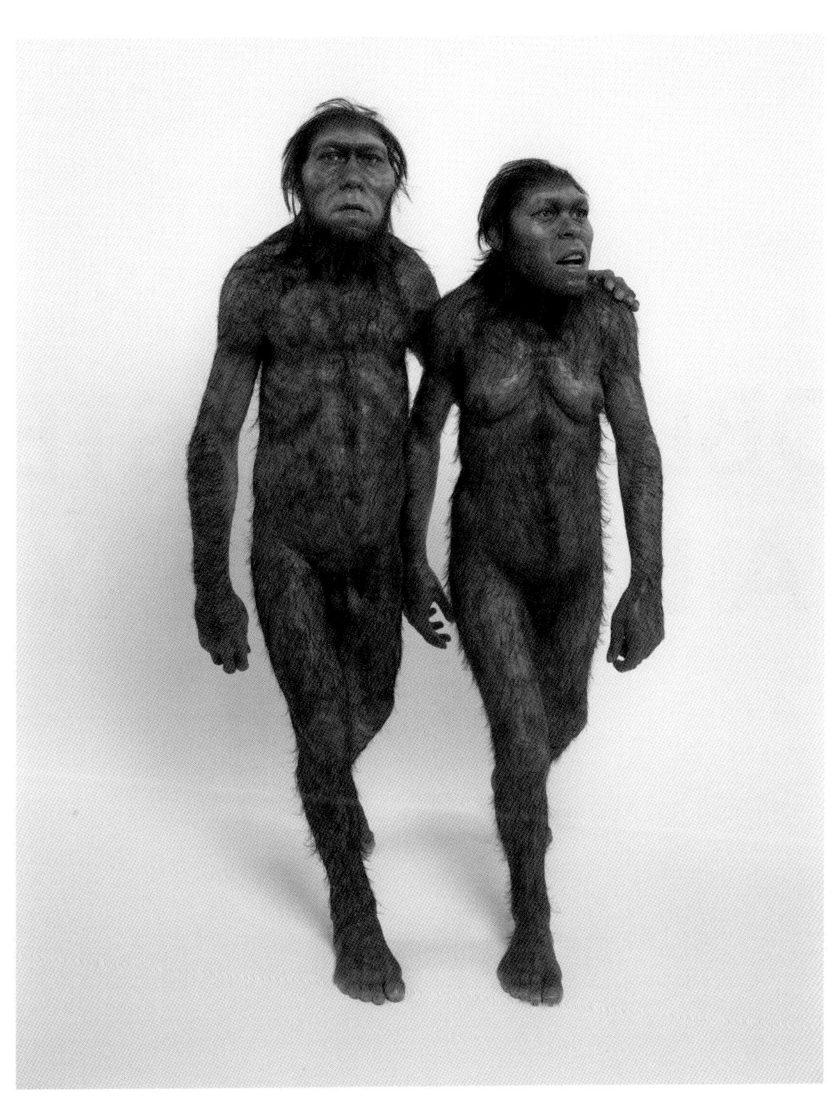

NOBLE & WEBSTER, A LOVE STORY

Linda Yablonsky

To understand the art of Tim Noble and Sue Webster is to know how much love has to do with it. The intensity of their personal relationship has been driving their collaboration for more than twenty years. You can see the feeling in their materials as well as their images—pulsating hearts, flowers, dollar signs, and their vulnerable, naked selves. If their assemblages start with the contents of trash bins and their light-bulb sculptures derive from the carnival midway, romance is at the bottom of all of it.

The two fell for each other in the mid-1980s as students at art school in Nottingham, in the East Midlands of England. Their attraction wasn't just physical. They shared the same belief in making sculpture with found materials. They also bonded over the post-punk music of the day, adopting both the sneering attitude and the dark aesthetic of the bands they followed, dyeing their hair black or bleaching it, and dressing in black with plenty of eye makeup. They looked like family.

Yet Webster has always been yin to Noble's yang. She's the pragmatist, he's the dreamer. If he had the vision, she made it real. They are counterweights. Every artwork they have made together is a marriage of opposites, at once chaotic and serene, comic and melancholy, cynical and celebratory. Many works literally have two faces. Not for these artists the passionless, hands-off, perfect fabrication. Noble and Webster mean to be confrontational.

Some people dislike this, and their criticism isn't mild. It's so kitschy, they say, or sentimental, or callous, or just too much—simplistic one-liners for the silly set. That may be true, as far as it goes, but it doesn't go far enough. With each exhibition, Noble and Webster touch another nerve. That's a healthy proposition for art. If it can't break the rules or rush the boundaries, if it can't make magic, it's not doing its job. But it's impossible to consider the Noble and Webster story without taking into account the lives behind it. If one wants to find meaning in what they do, that's where to look.

Webster grew up near Nottingham, in neighboring Leicester, the daughter of an electrician and a factory worker. She could draw and she could wire a lamp, but her only ambition was to be in a band. Touring punk bands regularly performed in Nottingham. Subject to wanderlust, Webster flew after them. In her neck of the woods, there was no future in art, but a woman could have a life in music. Going to art school, she says now, was "a way of killing time till my band kicked in."

Noble's parents were artists who lived in the countryside southwest of London. He was a tinkerer who spent much of his boyhood alone, improvising flying machines or lightning conductors. His parents took him to the Tate Gallery in London, where he saw the kinetic sculptures of Jean Tinguely, a huge influence. He knew he would be an artist. In college he also dreamed of being the singer in a band, but when he got up on stage and opened his mouth, nothing came out. Like Webster, he was better with his hands.

Assemblage came to Webster naturally, but not until she tried her luck as a painter. Tripping on LSD at a summer music festival, she started seeing in 3-D. The following fall she switched from painting to sculpture and trusted her instincts. They led her outside, where she started collecting objects and incorporating them in sculptures inspired by what she saw in her head. Noble was still making motorized sculptures, much as he had as a boy, working from his imagination and, like Webster, composing with whatever was lying around.

As undergraduates Noble and Webster didn't make art together, but they traveled together. After watching *Midnight Express*, Webster proposed a trip to Istanbul. On arrival she attracted attention from men who were charmed by her skimpy dress and bleached blond hair, and hisses from women for the same reason. Dispensing with the usual tourist sights, she and Noble scoured junkyards, looking for scraps to bring back to their studios at college.

Oddly, Istanbul was full of American cars and appliances—Chevrolets and refrigerators left by American soldiers years before. Webster fell in love again, this time with the idea of touring America. The following summer, with money from a travel grant that Noble won, the couple went from New York to Los Angeles on a Greyhound bus. They were on the road for a month. Wherever they stopped they picked up metal scraps and souvenirs to take back to their studios. Las Vegas was a bonanza of bright lights that created dramatic shadows. It left a deep impression that would later materialize in their signature artworks—flashing electric signs and shadow sculptures.

The bus trip set a precedent for later hunting and gathering expeditions that would take Noble and Webster to every continent in the world, and provide them with a piece of each—even Antarctica, from which they brought home a single pebble. "Antarctica," Noble says, "is pure minimalism."

In 1989, after graduation, the pair didn't
go to London as most art students around
them did. They went north to Yorkshire, to
Bradford, a crime-ridden, post-industrial city
near Leeds, where they could live cheaply and
maintain an enormous studio. Bradford had
scrap piles the size of buildings. The place
seemed made for them. It was there that their
collaboration as artists began.

Combining Webster's facility for electric
wiring with Noble's predilection for kinetic
objects proved fortuitous. The two earned a
living by creating stage sets and props for
Ecstasy-fueled rave concerts. At last they were
no longer starstruck spectators. They were
with the bands. Yet in 1992, after a residency
at the Henry Moore Studio in Dean Clough—
a place for high art, not spontaneity—their
pleasure in the rave scene was diminishing.
They needed a challenge. That's when they
heard that an artist in London had exhibited
a dead shark in a tank of formaldehyde. They
drove two hundred miles to see this shark. It
scared the shit out of them. Conceptualism
and weighty subjects like sex and mortality
had been missing from their formal vocabu-
lary. Clearly it was time to move to London.
A sensational new generation—Damien Hirst,
Tracey Emin, Gary Hume, Sarah Lucas—was on

the scene. "It was like when punk exploded," Webster says. "It wiped out everything else."

Both Noble and Webster applied to the Royal College of Art. Only Noble was admitted but he was given a subsidized flat and the couple lived in it for two years. A friend from school introduced them to Joshua Constant, a young dealer in the East End who staged carnival-like events in the street outside his gallery. Hirst and Angus Fairhurst, dressed as clowns, made spin paintings. Emin organized a roulette game with a spinning office chair. Noble and Webster were entranced. The following year Constant invited them to participate. That was their entrance into the art world.

Now they were in the thick of things but they needed a place to work. The East End was Jack the Ripper territory, rough and desolate. Perfect for them. It had scores of empty warehouses. Noble and Webster moved into one, on Rivington Street, where they started making sculpture with the materials at hand—their lives, their bodies, their ardor, and their scatological sense of humor. (Even now, their website greets visitors with "Welcome Motherfuckers.")

The year was 1996 and they started making sculptures of pulsating lights that Webster wired herself. The first was a cartoony, six-foot-tall fountain whose bright lights appeared to bubble and spark. Titled *Excessive Sexual Indulgence* it more than hinted at the circulation of bodily fluids, but it didn't look anything like the work that the Young British Artists—Hirst and Emin and the rest—were turning out. Noble and Webster's art was obvious, colorful, dirty-mouthed, and shot through with a mania that loudly announced their presence.

The couple went on to make marqueelike signs that spelled out affirmative words and phrases such as *Forever, I ♥ YOU*, and *YE$*, but which carried the threat of extinction with every flip of the switch. Nothing lasts forever. Practically a taunt, love is intimate and tender, yet the appropriated image—a glowing heart substituted for "love"—appears on throwaway plastic shopping bags all over New York City.

Noble and Webster's sculptures turn on a critical contradiction. In this case, the work makes a travesty of sincerity, while the dollar symbol that forms the "s" in *YE$* (2001) points to the base profit motive of a sales pitch in even the most positive utterance. Nonetheless, there's something sexy in the heat of the lights, and sex, that most basic of all human activities, is something that Noble and Webster promote in drawings, paintings, signage, and

sculpture with an abandon so aggressive it vio-
lates their own privacy, like the animist mass
of black rubber dildos that forms the comical
shadow portrait *Black Narcissus* (2006). That is
nasty. It's beautiful. It's honest.

The light sculptures took time and involved
other people. To amuse themselves, Noble
and Webster started fiddling with all the
stuff in the studio, not just their memora-
bilia but their rubbish. Soon they had
Dirty White Trash (with Gulls) (1998), their
first "shadow" work—their first child, in a way,
Webster says. In the light of day it appears
to be an overflowing pile of refuse, so wicked
that two seagulls have fallen dead from it. Yet
this is one of Noble and Webster's most personal self-portraits. The trash was not picked
from anonymous bins. It's *their* trash—their
discarded boxes of hair dye and soda cans,
their crushed cigarette packs and rolls of toi-
let paper, the wrappers of food they ate—all
consumed in the studio over six months. The
seagulls? Noble's father collected taxidermy.

Point a light projector at the pile and, in a
stroke of legerdemain, the shadows cast on
the wall are articulate renderings of the two
artists sitting back-to-back, lifting a glass
and smoking. "It was made of *us*," Webster
says of the sculpture, virtually a memory

piece, "of the stuff that kept us alive while we were making it." If unconventional, *Dirty White Trash (with Gulls)* has the verisimilitude of traditional portraiture. So much so that it's tempting to propose Noble and Webster as hardcore realists, or practiced illusionists. But the work also has roots in process art, scatter art, and Pop Art. It's a conceptual feint as well, self-mocking, self-validating, and seeded with an irreverence that doubles as devotion. "If you're in love," Noble says, "it's very passionate, it's very key, it's very focused. It's your source material and it's volatile. Sparks fly."

Even more charged is *Masters of the Universe*, a figurative wax sculpture from 2000 that is shocking in its grossness. The figures are life-size Neanderthals out of a natural history museum diorama, or perhaps outcasts from *Planet of the Apes*. They are covered in human body hair and seem lost in a white void, two defiant souls with the grimacing faces of Noble and Webster. Alone in the world, they're masters of nothing and also everything that exists, a snub to the idealized bodies common to art and fashion. They're frightening.

By 2001 Noble and Webster were living in The Dirty House, a bunkerlike warehouse in Shoreditch converted by David Adjaye into an immense studio with a luxurious penthouse on top. In 2008 Noble and Webster got married on the *Queen Elizabeth* in a ceremony conducted by Tracey Emin. The newlyweds had made a typically rude, wonderfully ebullient red neon, *fuckingbeautiful*, but the marriage was partly a salvage operation. Their relationship was falling apart. Four years later Noble and Webster split up. The creative collaboration, however, continues. As Noble says, "It's always interesting to turn your life upside down." Webster adds, "Something new will come out of it."

WORKS

50 Ways to Leave Your Lover, 1996

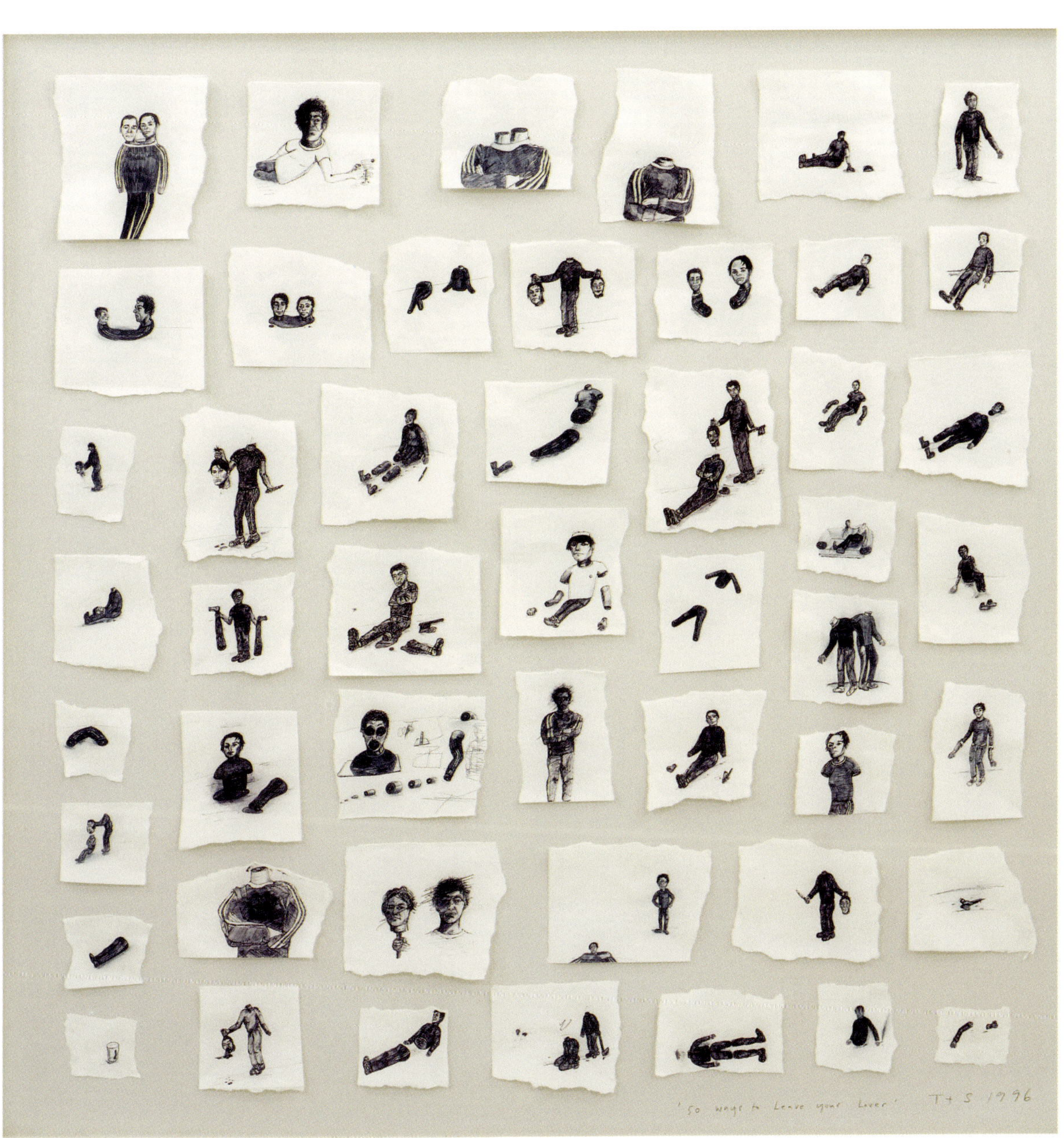
'50 ways to Leave your Lover'   T + S 1996

Excessive Sensual Indulgence, 1996

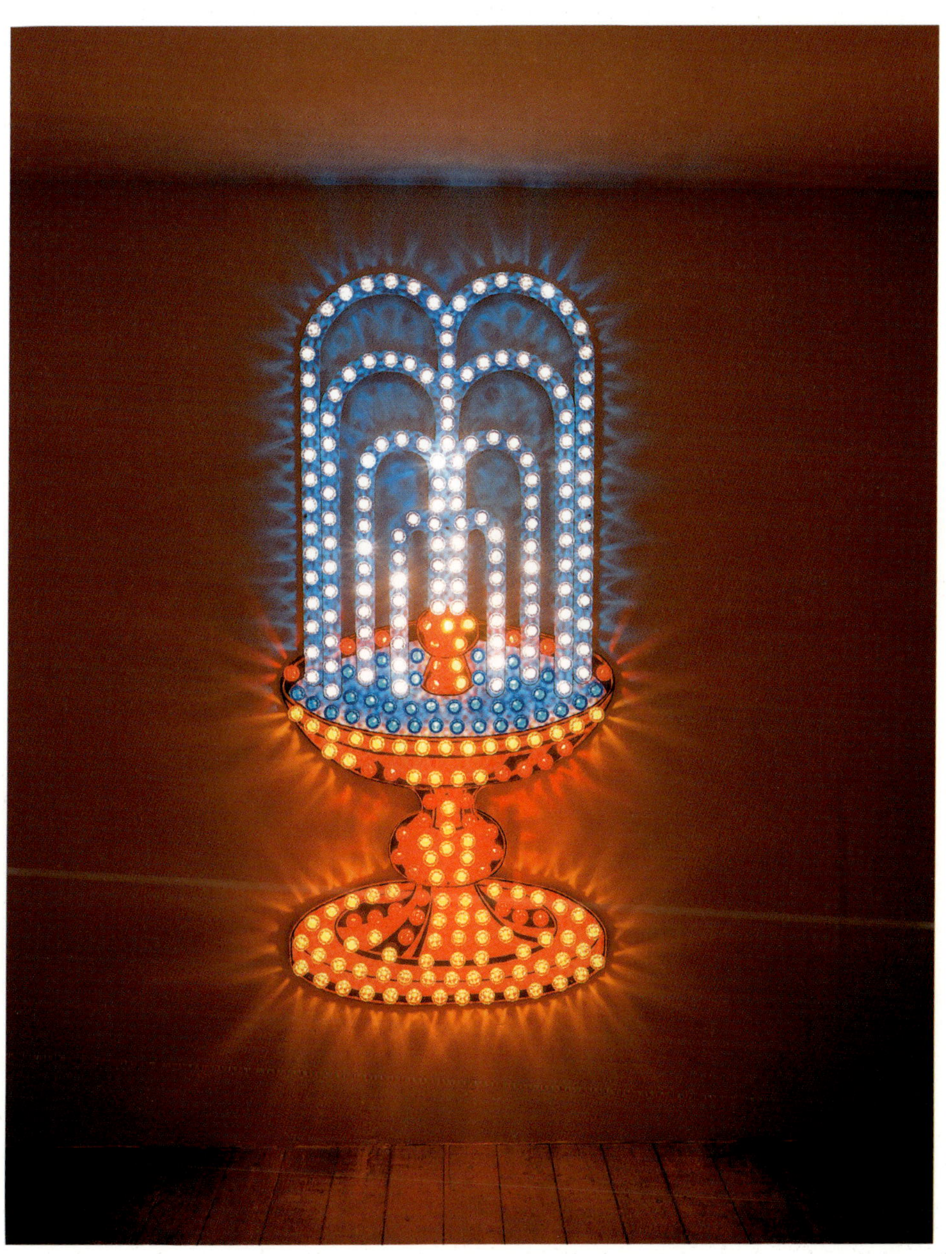

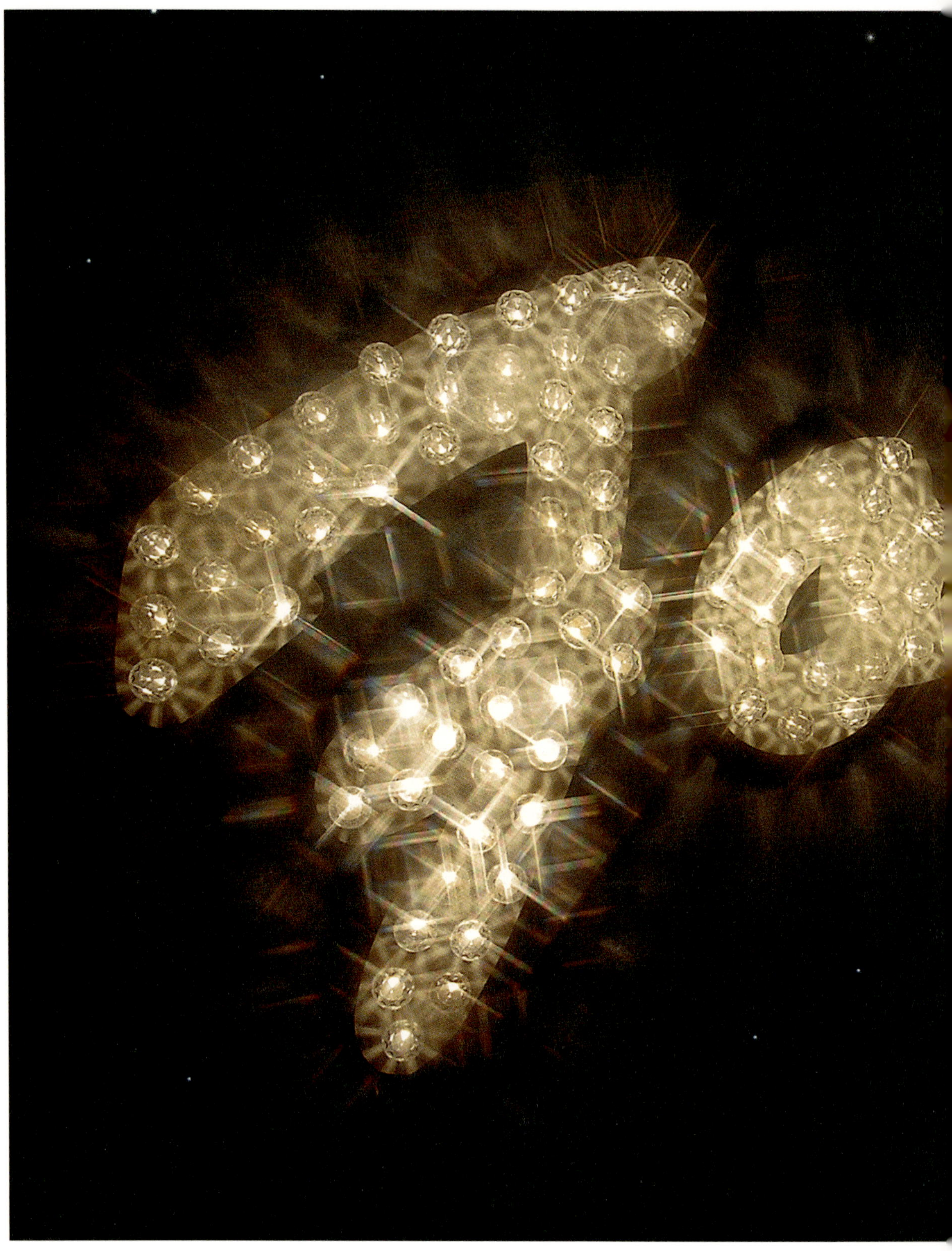

Forever, 1996

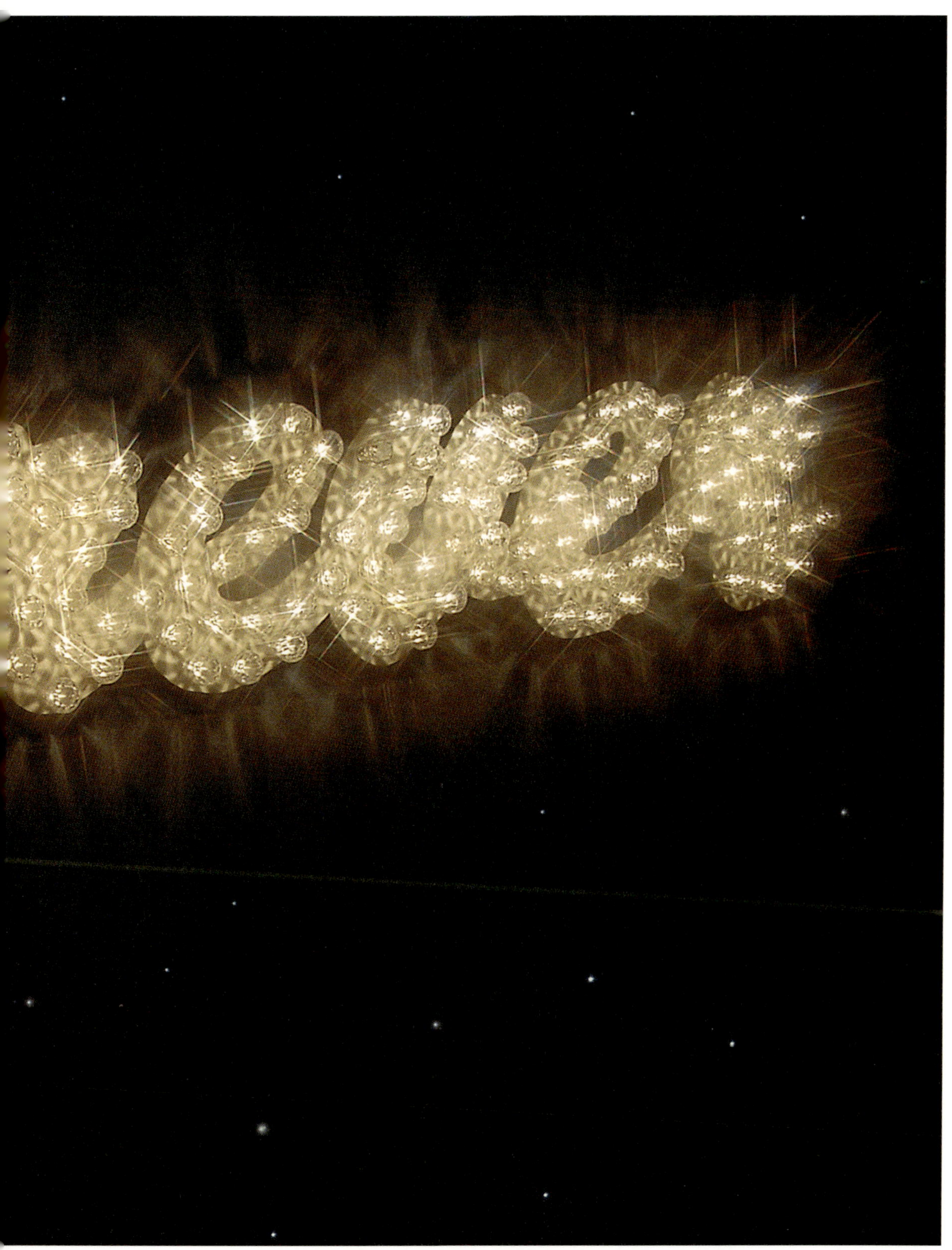

London Swings (poster), 1997

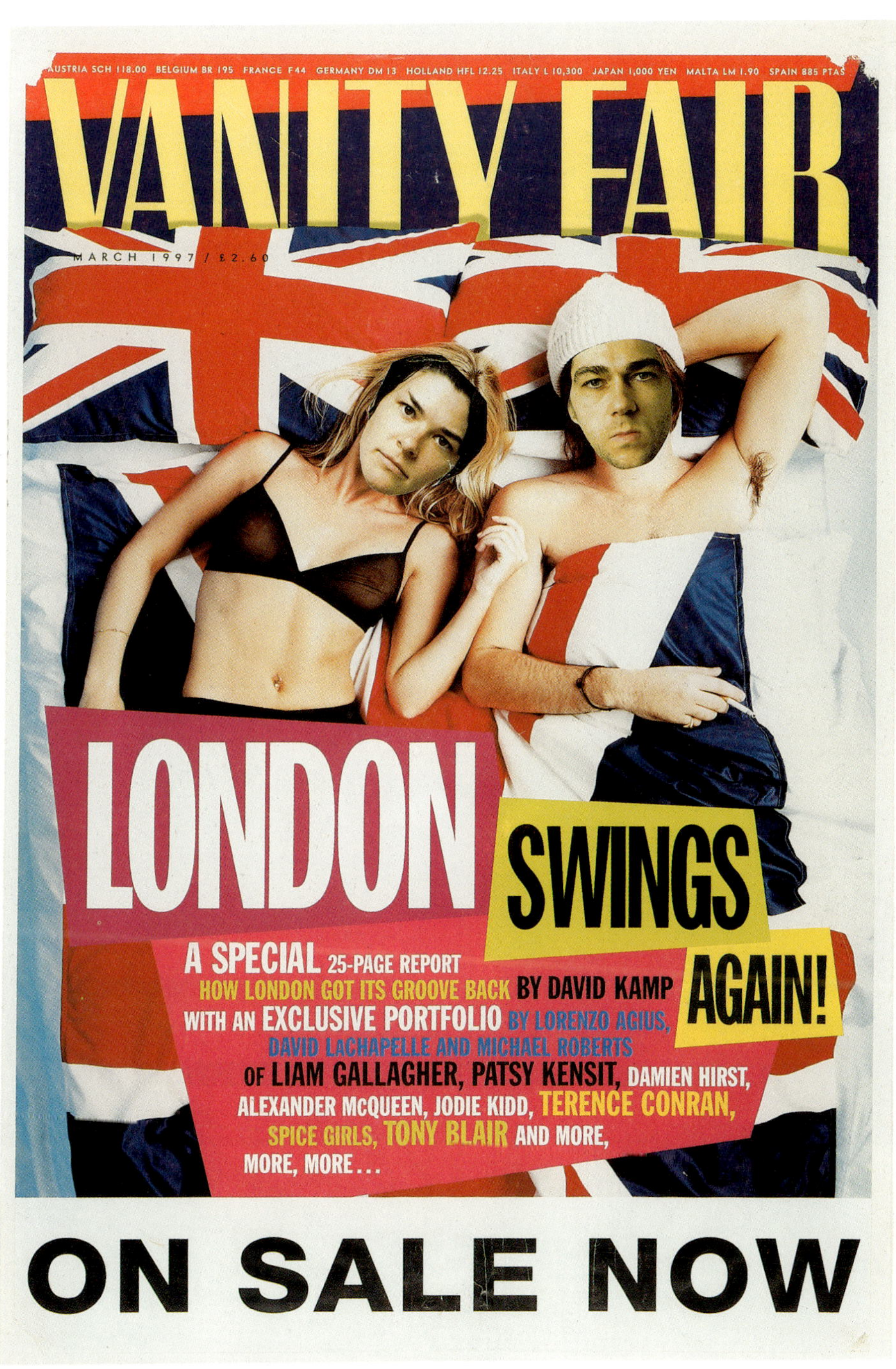

AUSTRIA SCH 118.00   BELGIUM BR 195   FRANCE F44   GERMANY DM 13   HOLLAND HFL 12.25   ITALY L 10,300   JAPAN 1,000 YEN   MALTA LM 1.90   SPAIN 885 PTAS
VANITY FAIR
MARCH 1997 / £2.60
LONDON
SWINGS
AGAIN!
A SPECIAL 25-PAGE REPORT
HOW LONDON GOT ITS GROOVE BACK BY DAVID KAMP
WITH AN EXCLUSIVE PORTFOLIO BY LORENZO AGIUS,
DAVID LACHAPELLE AND MICHAEL ROBERTS
OF LIAM GALLAGHER, PATSY KENSIT, DAMIEN HIRST,
ALEXANDER McQUEEN, JODIE KIDD, TERENCE CONRAN,
SPICE GIRLS, TONY BLAIR AND MORE,
MORE, MORE . . .
ON SALE NOW

Dirty White Trash (with Gulls), 1998

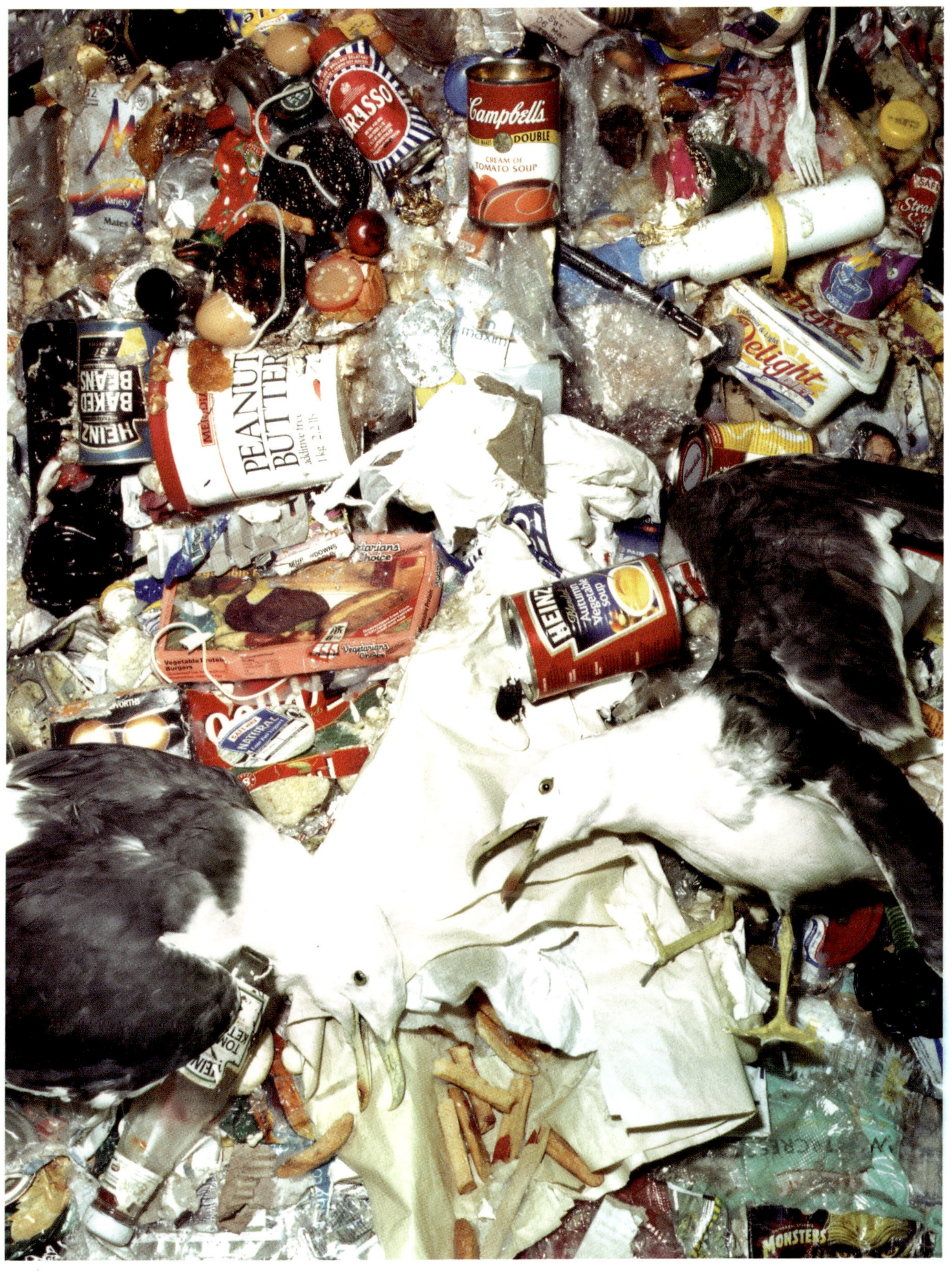

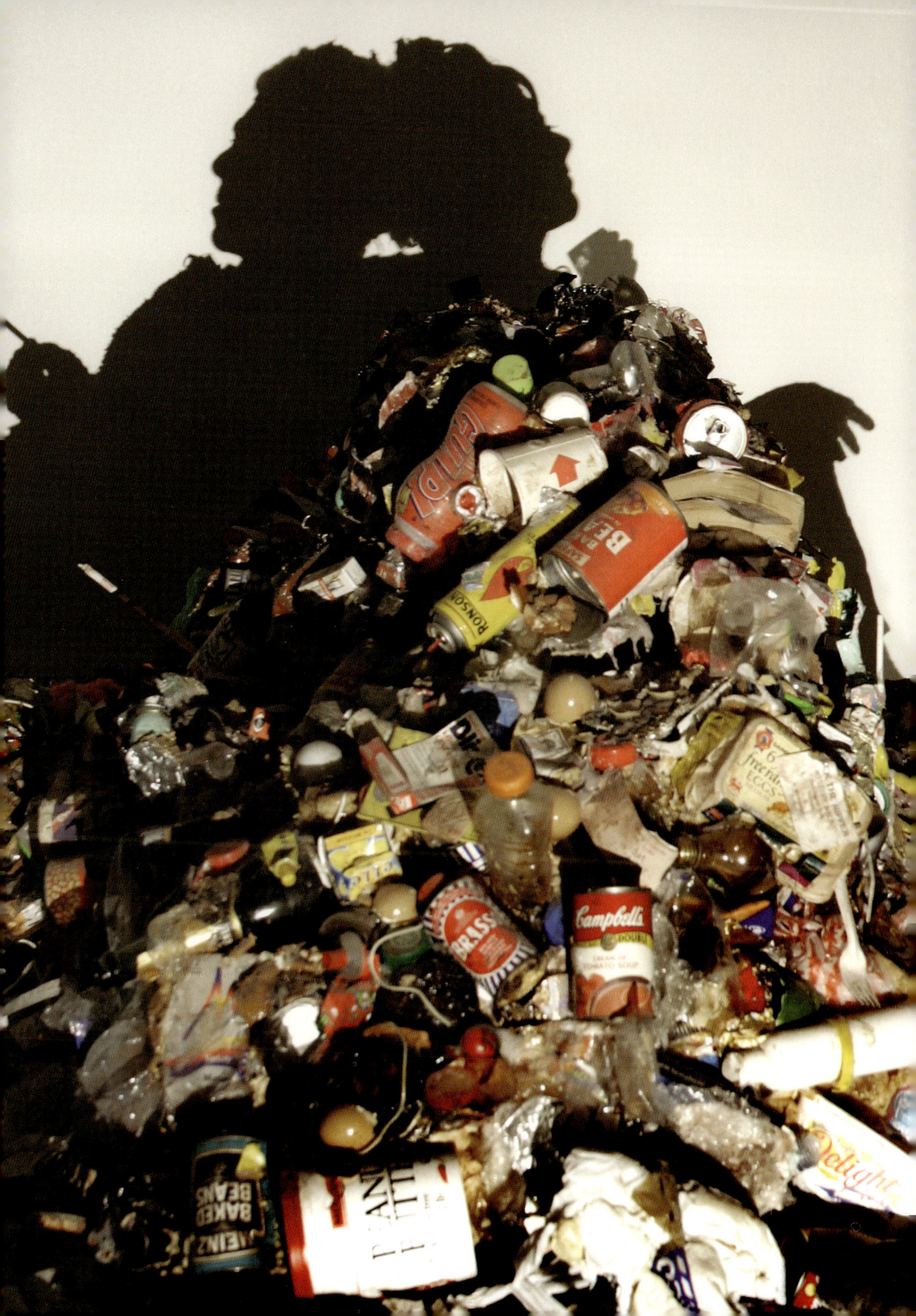

Simply Natural, 1999

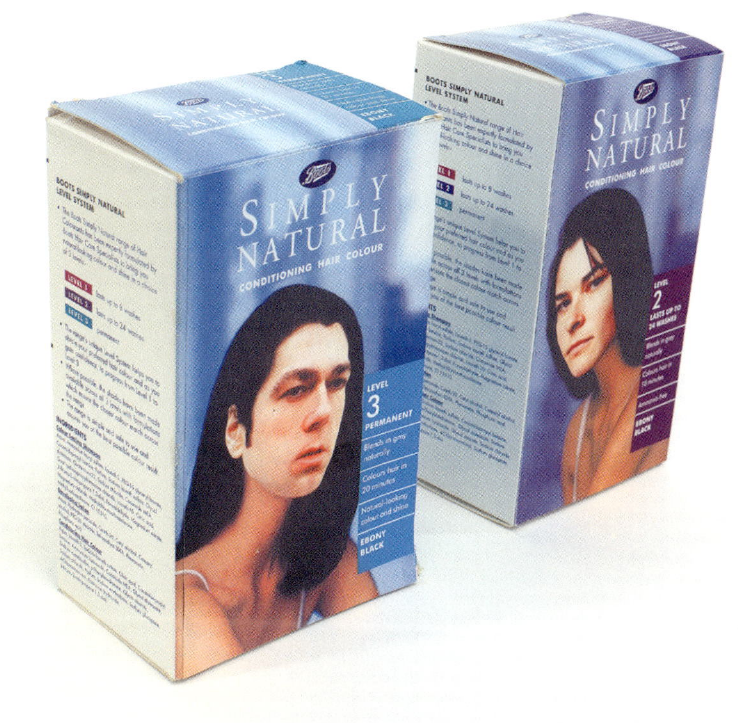
BOOTS SIMPLY NATURAL
LEVEL SYSTEM

Boots
SIMPLY
NATURAL
CONDITIONING HAIR COLOUR

LEVEL 1
LEVEL 2
LEVEL 3

LEVEL
3
PERMANENT

Blends in grey
naturally

Colours hair in
20 minutes

Natural-looking
colour and shine

EBONY
BLACK

BOOTS SIMPLY NATURAL
LEVEL SYSTEM

Boots
SIMPLY
NATURAL
CONDITIONING HAIR COLOUR

LEVEL 1
LEVEL 2
LEVEL 3

LEVEL
2
LASTS UP TO
24 WASHES

Blends in grey
naturally

Colours hair in
20 minutes

Ammonia-free

EBONY
BLACK

From F**k to Trash, 2000

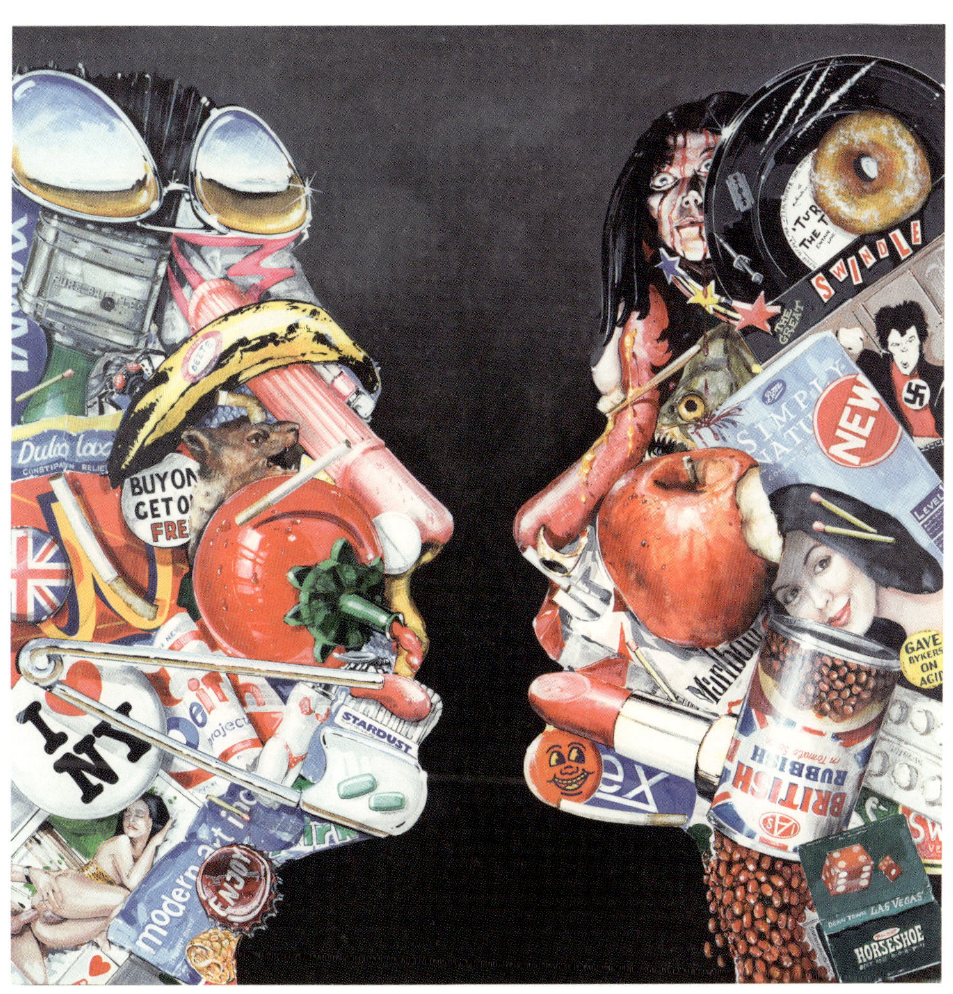

Masters of the Universe, 2000

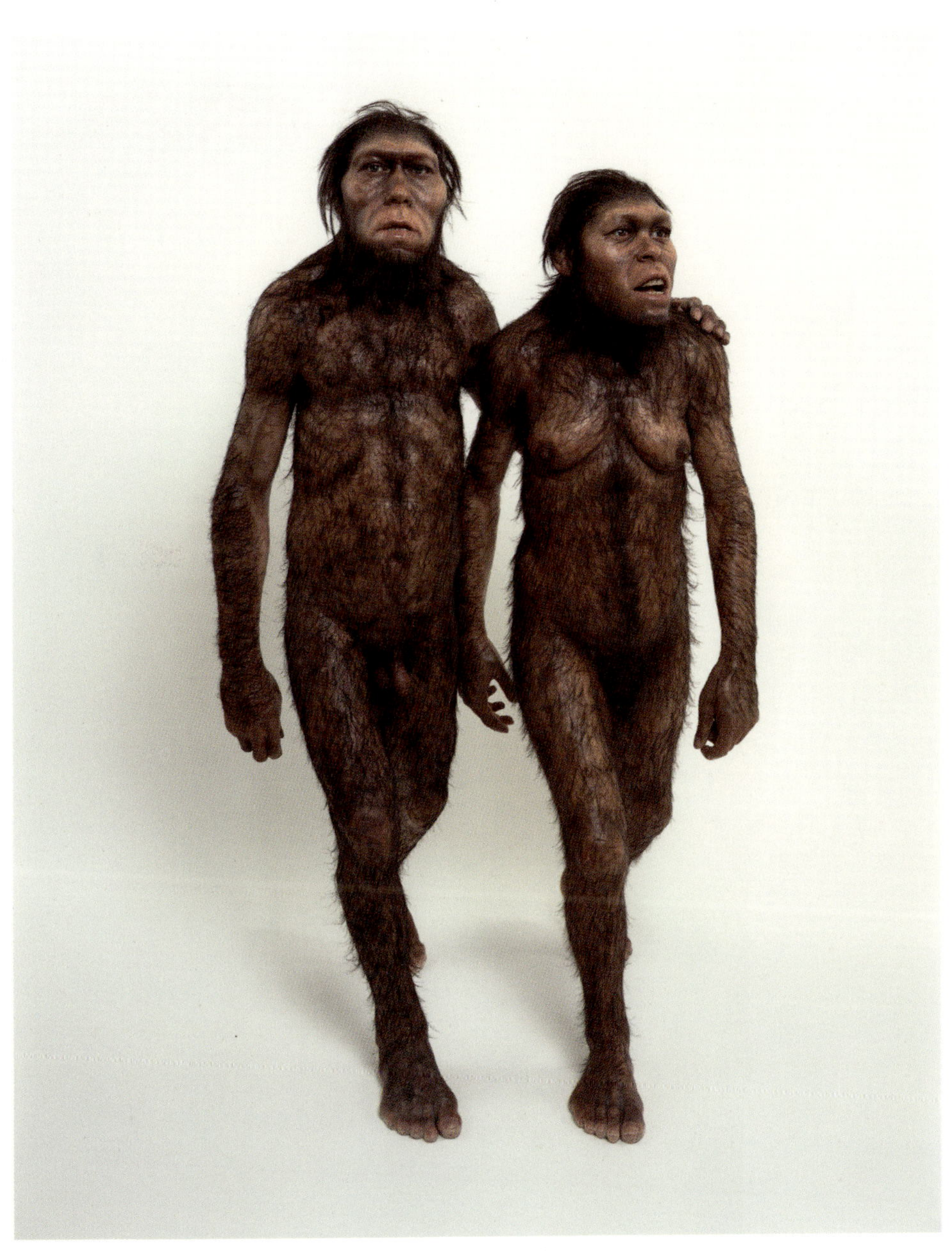

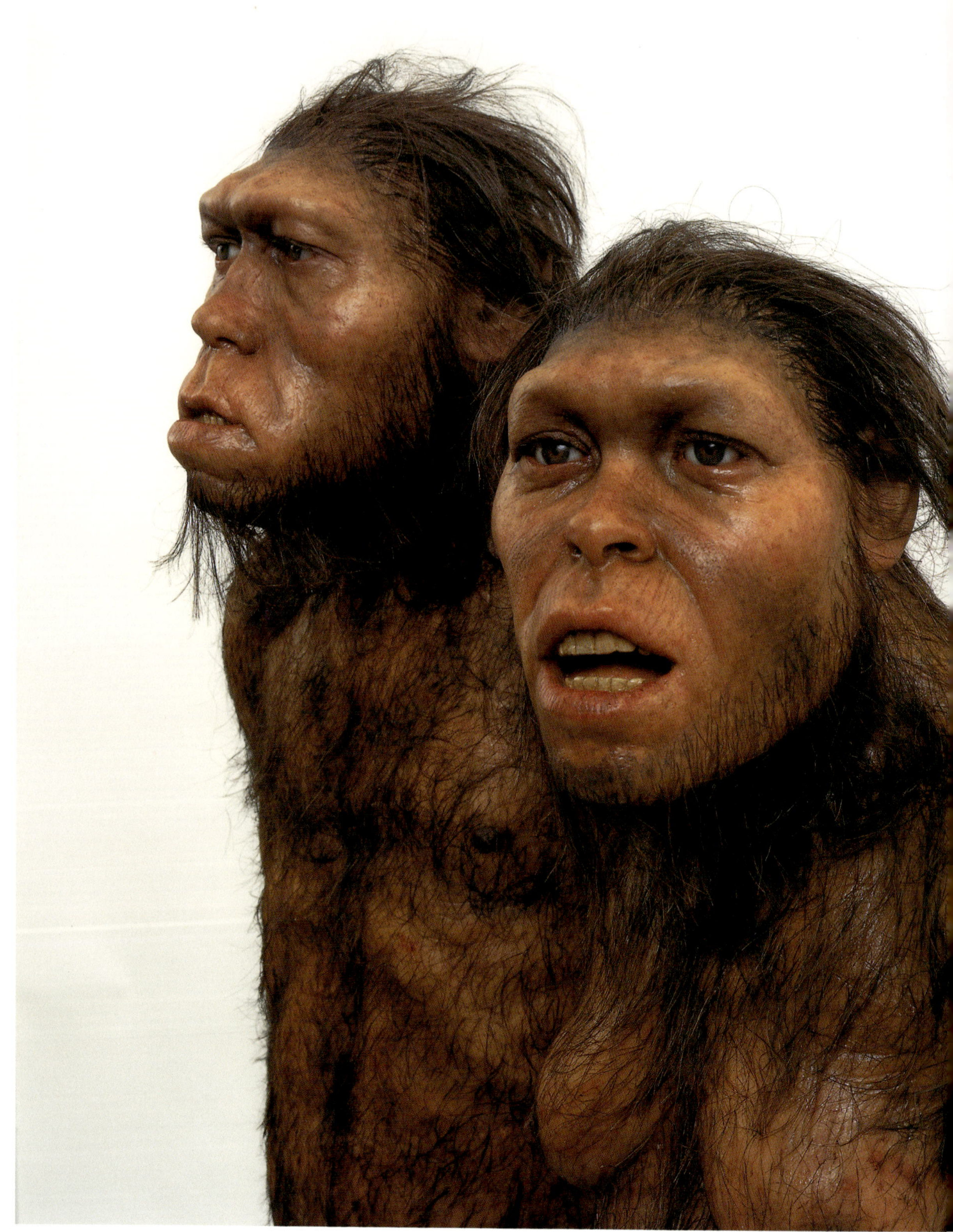

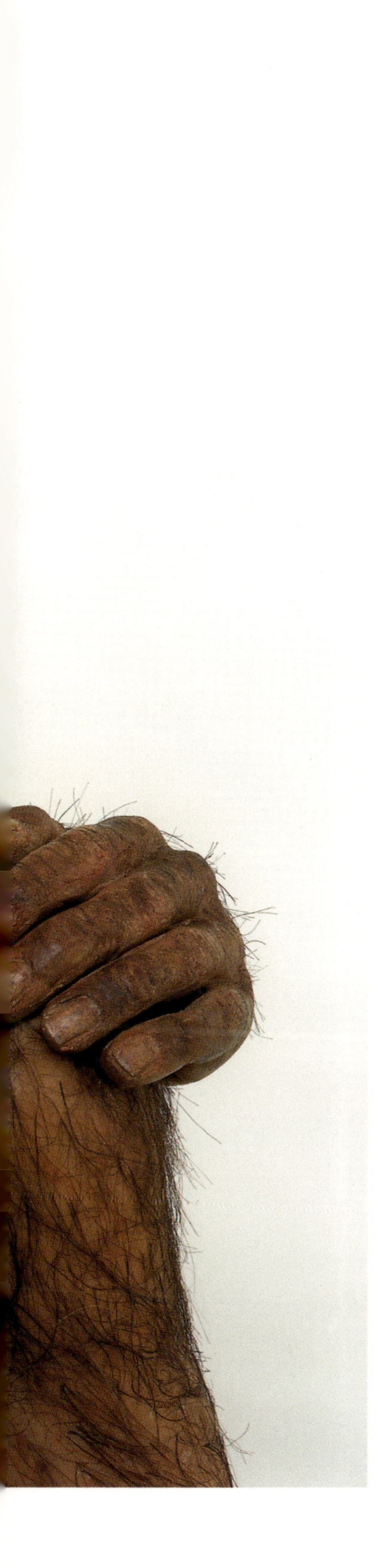

The Original Sinners, 2000

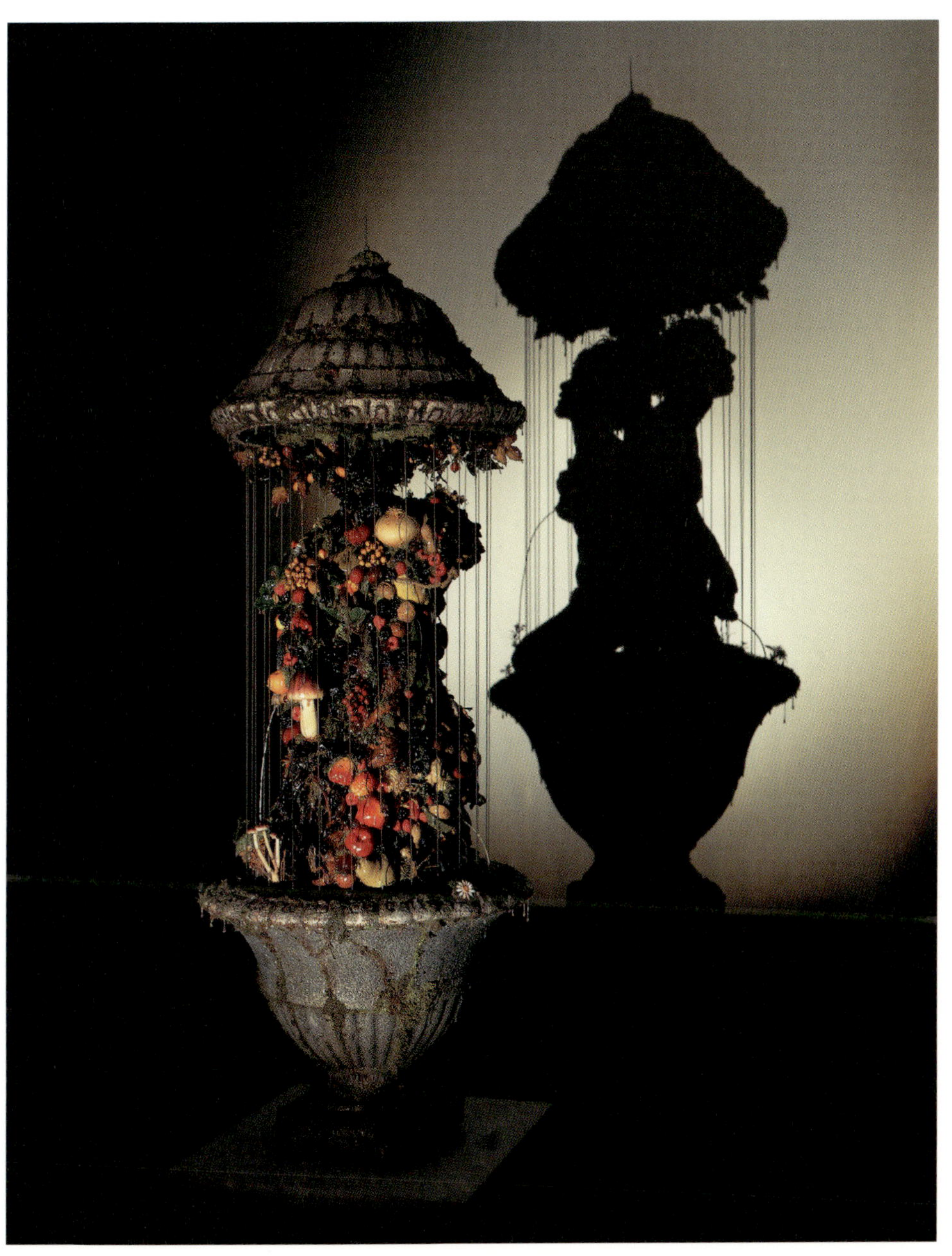

I (Heart) YOU (I LOVE YOU), 2000

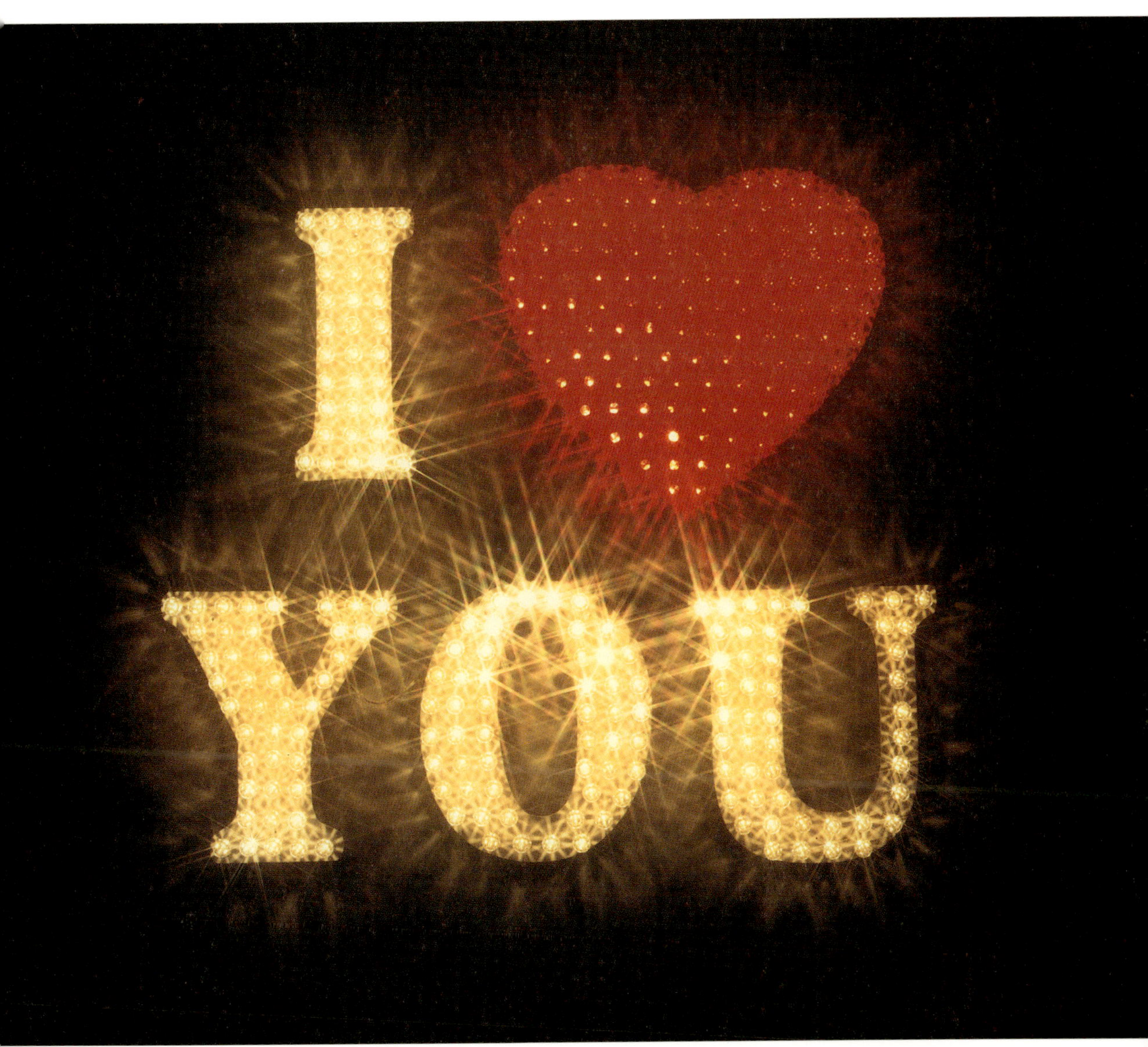

I ♥
YOU

YE$, 2001

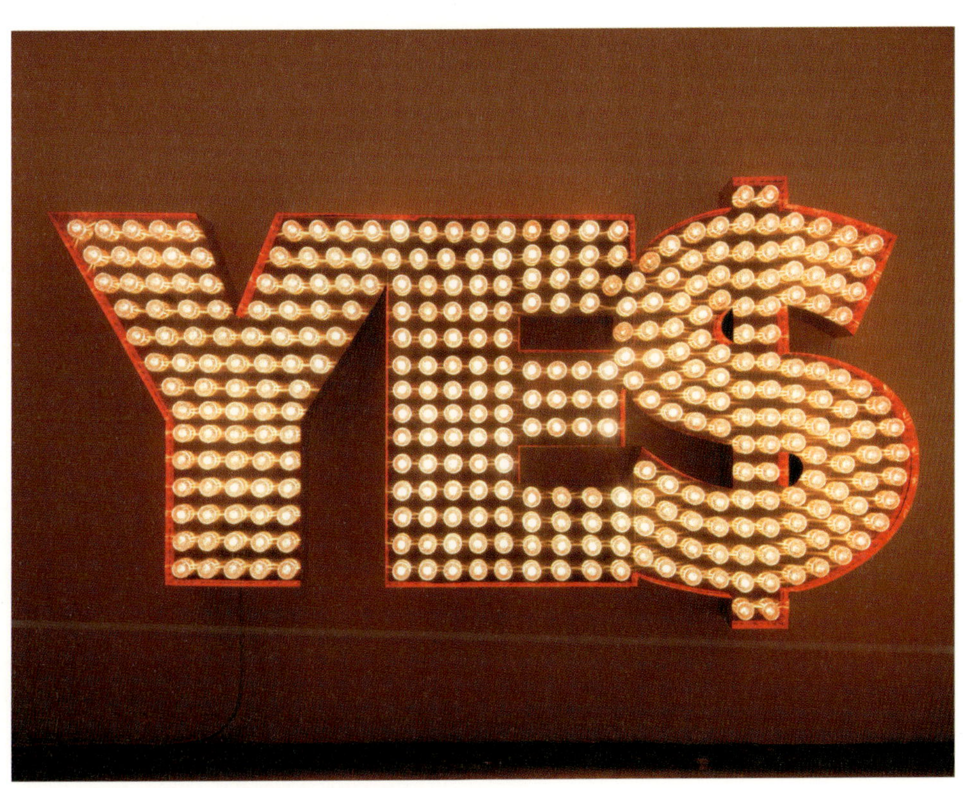
YE$

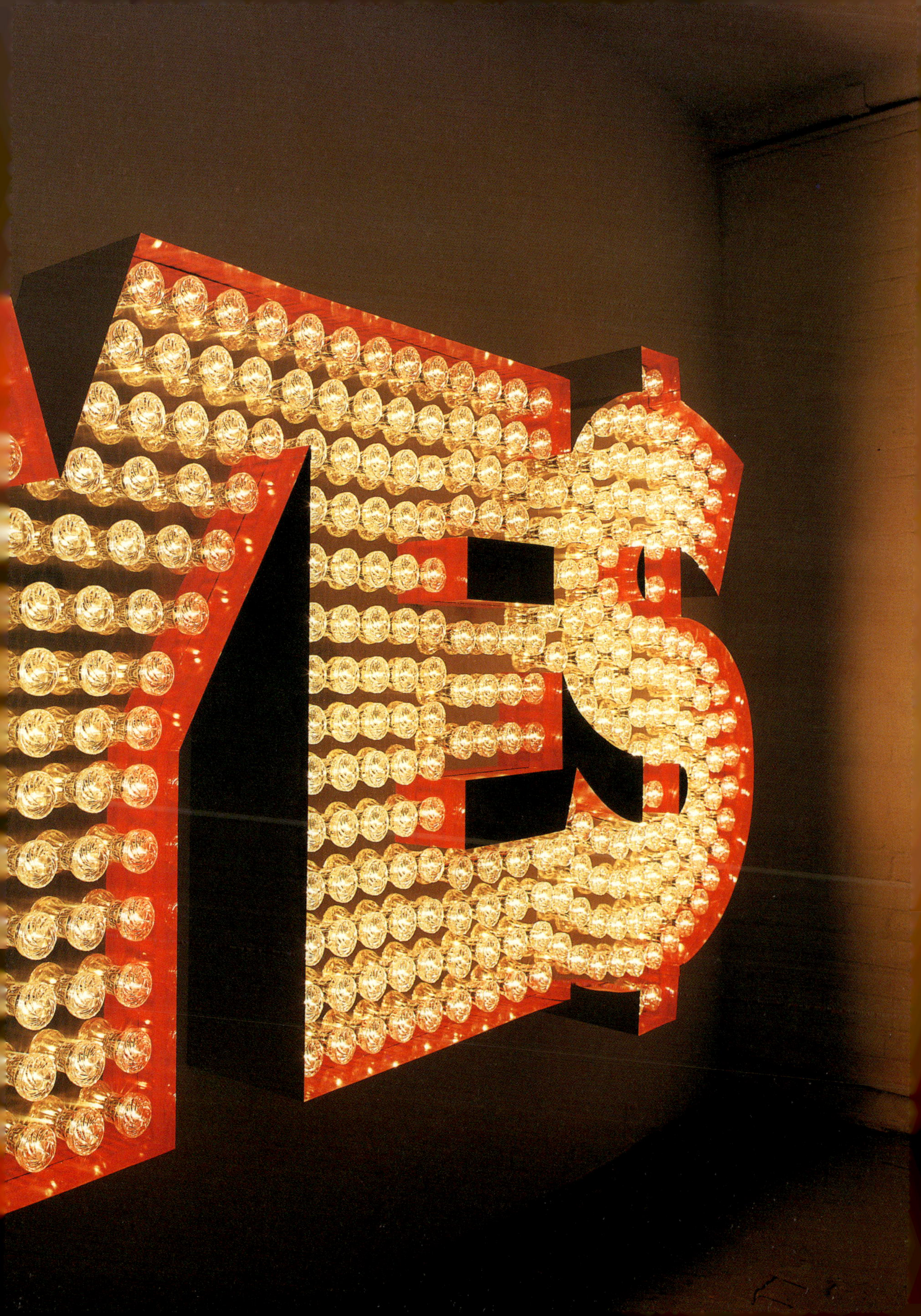

Lets Fuck, 2001

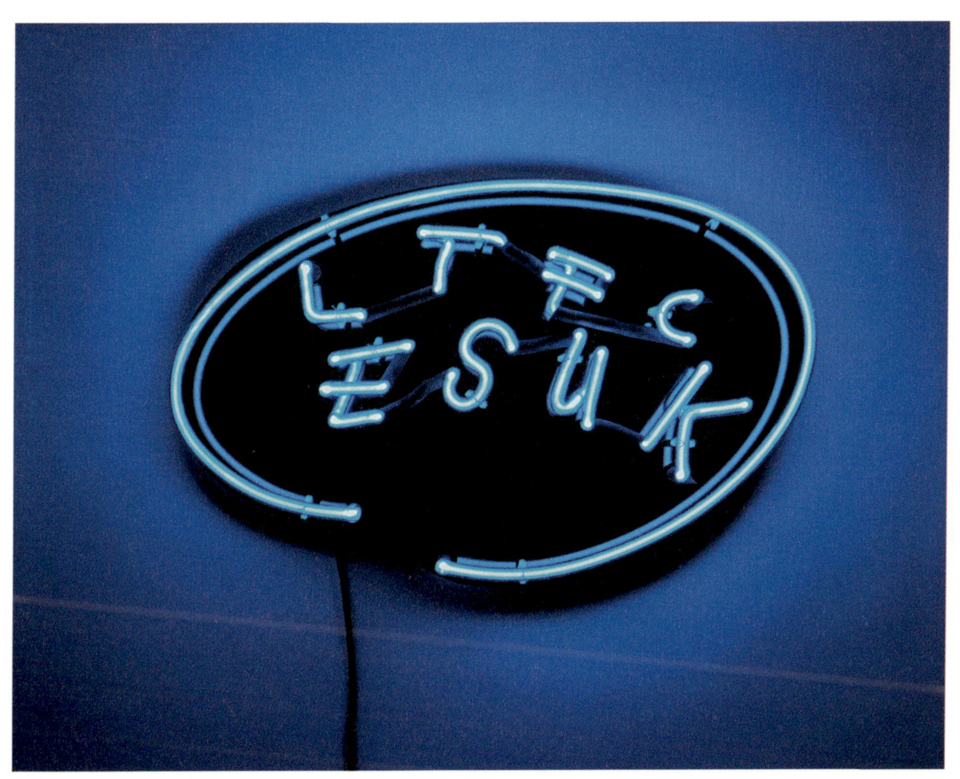

49

I Love Sex, 2002

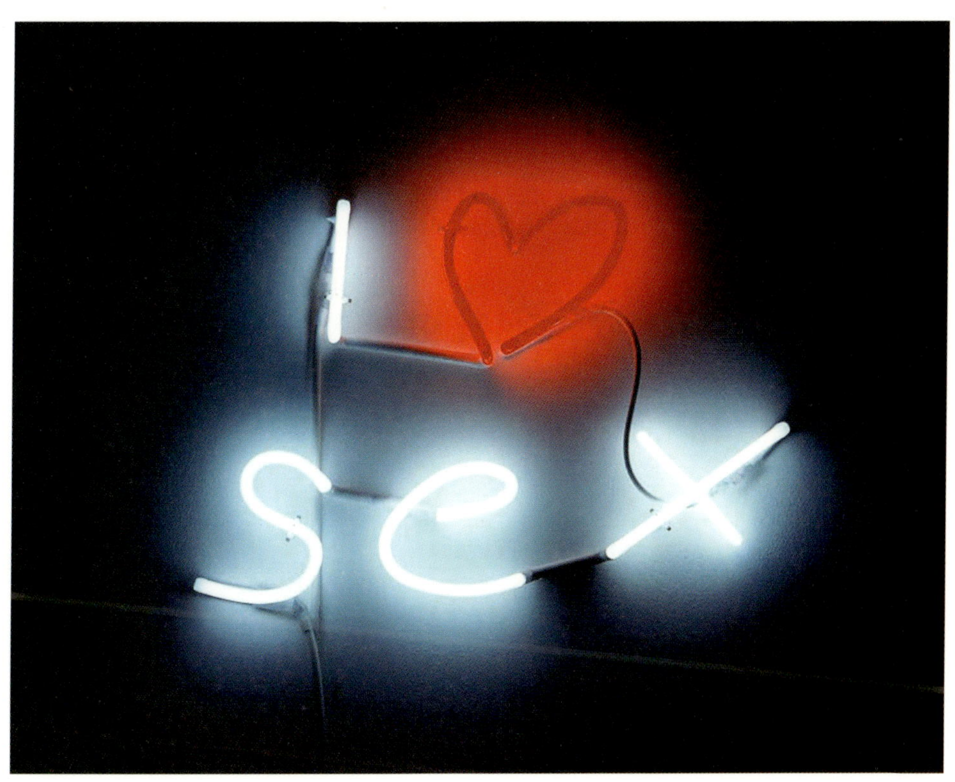
I ♥
sex

Black Magic Paintings Series, 2002

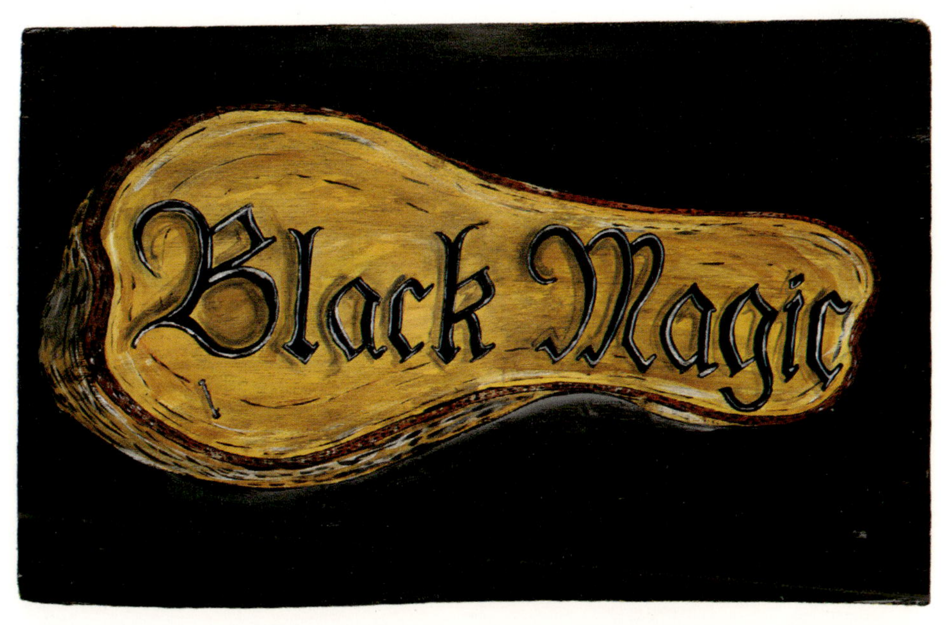

Black Magic

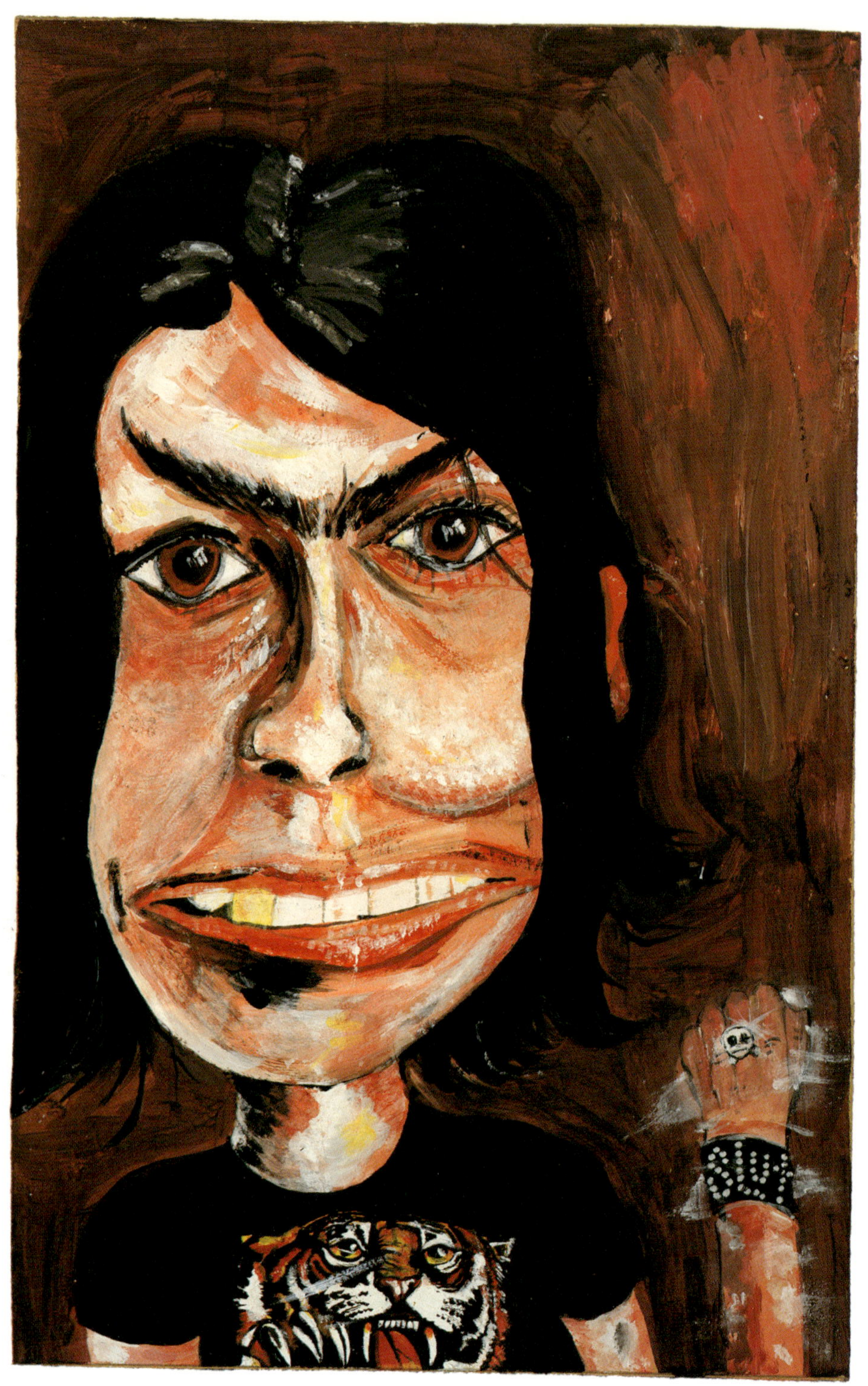

Sue By Tim

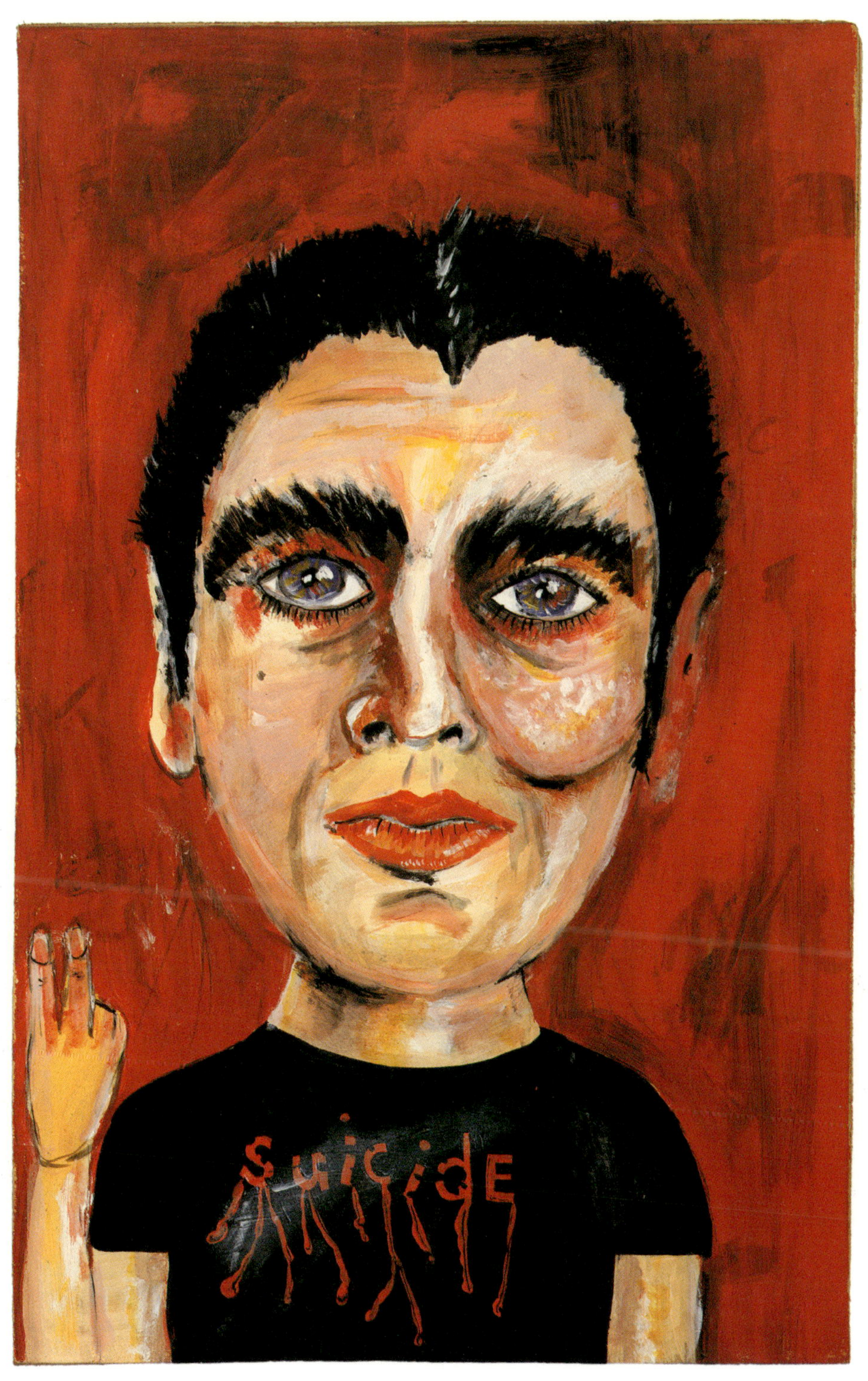

Tim By Sue

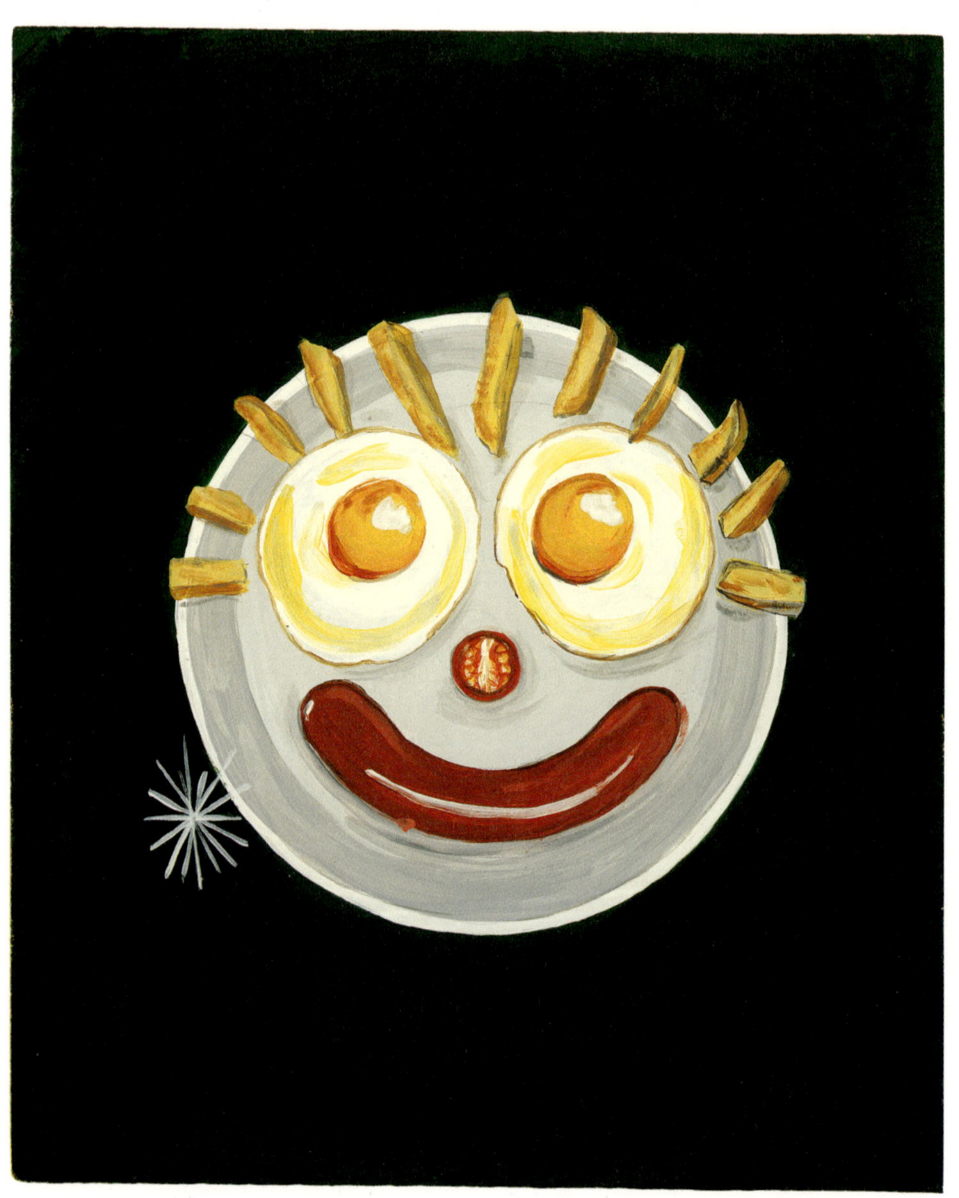

Happy Meal

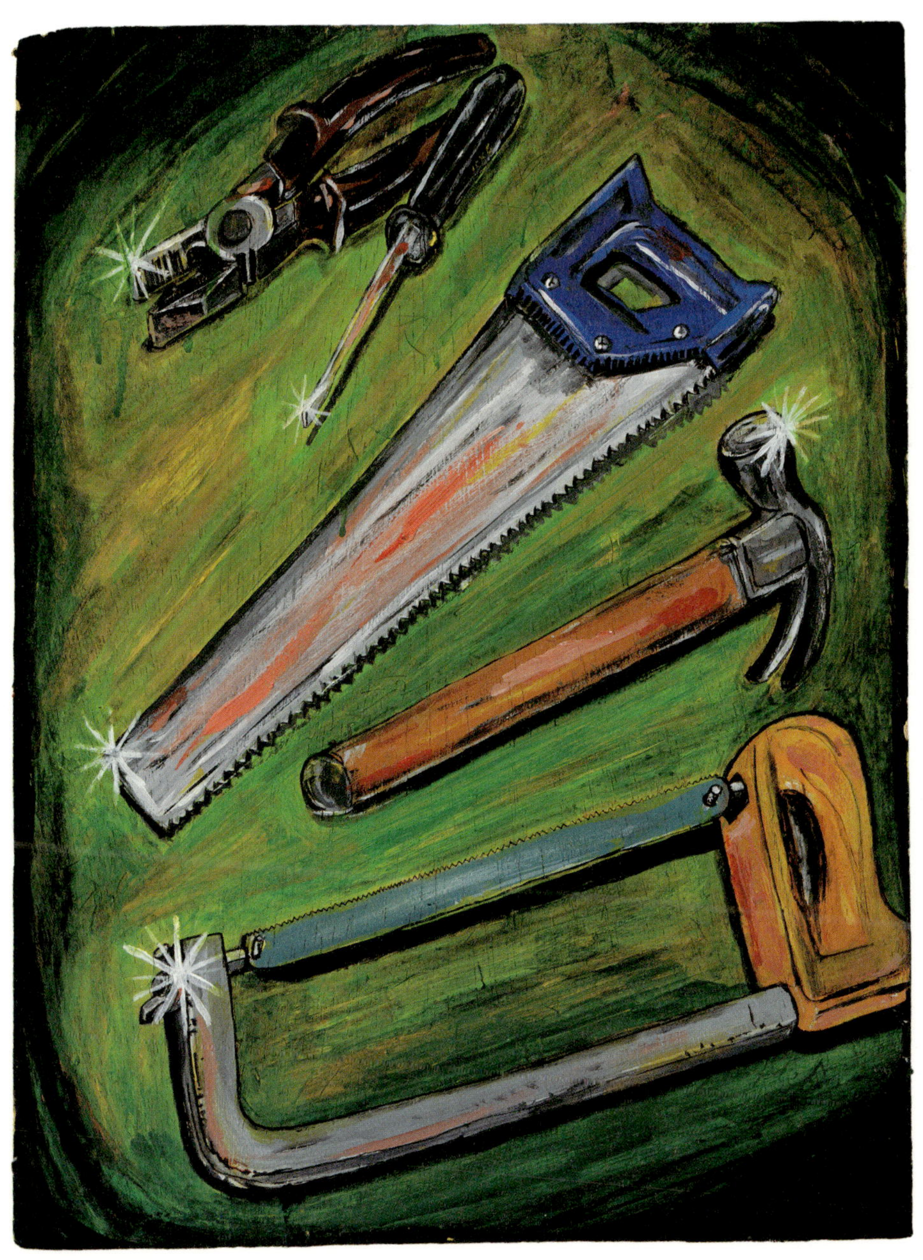

Tool Kit

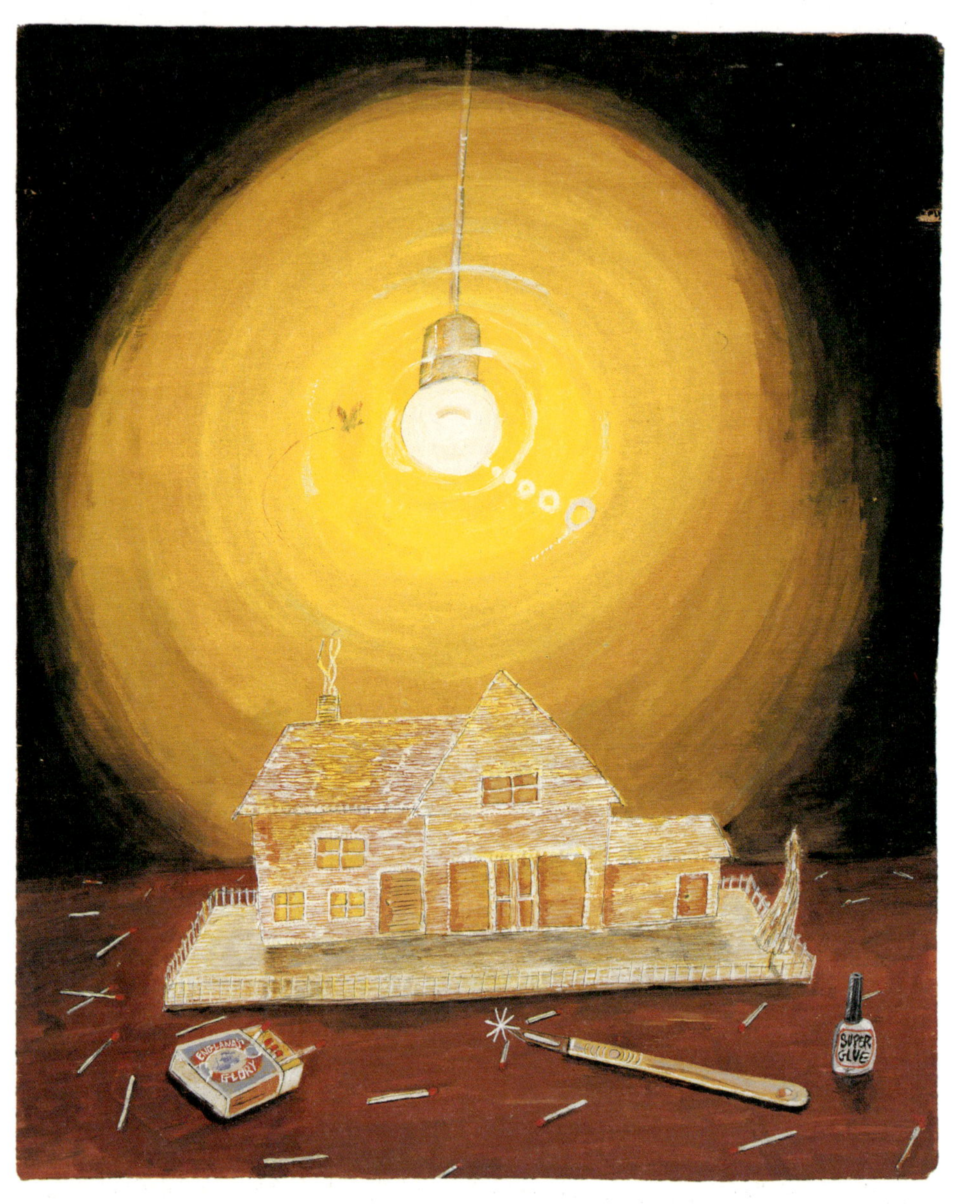

Matchstick House

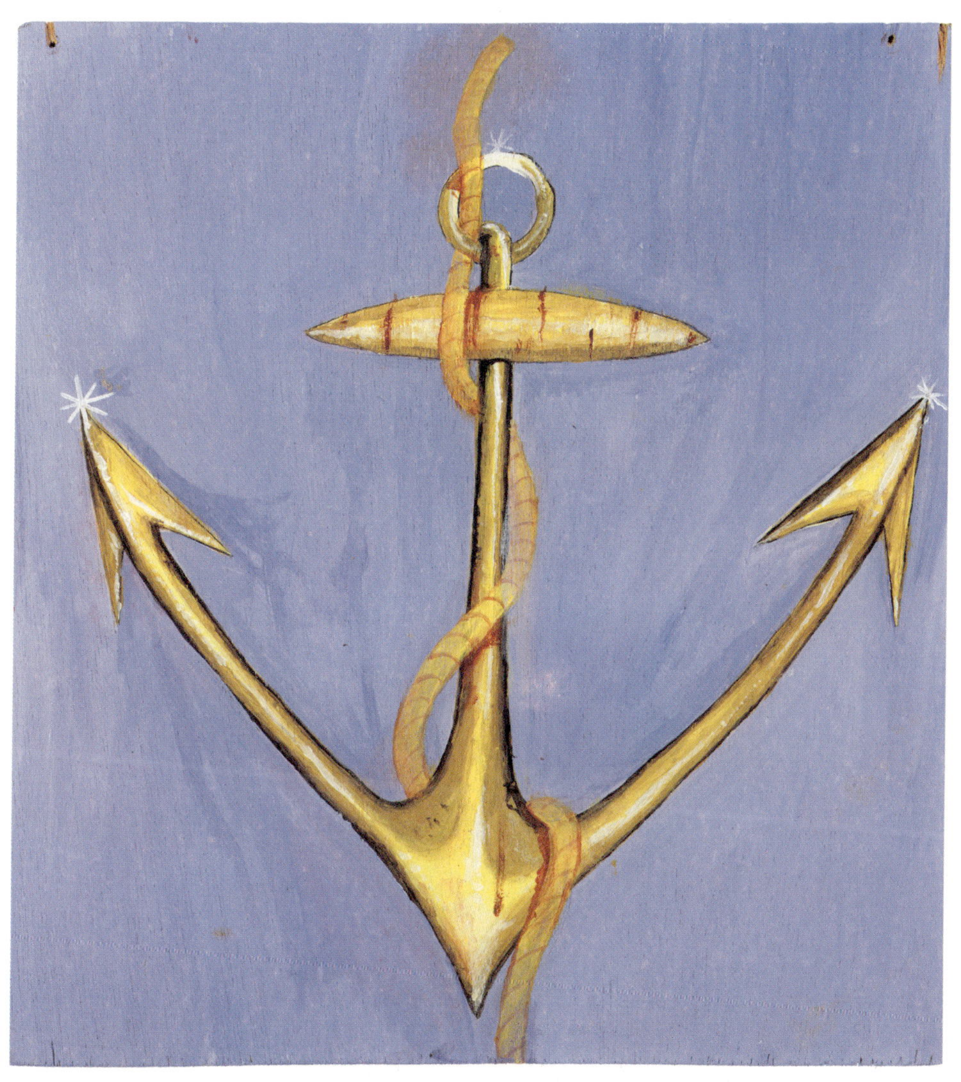

Blue Anchor

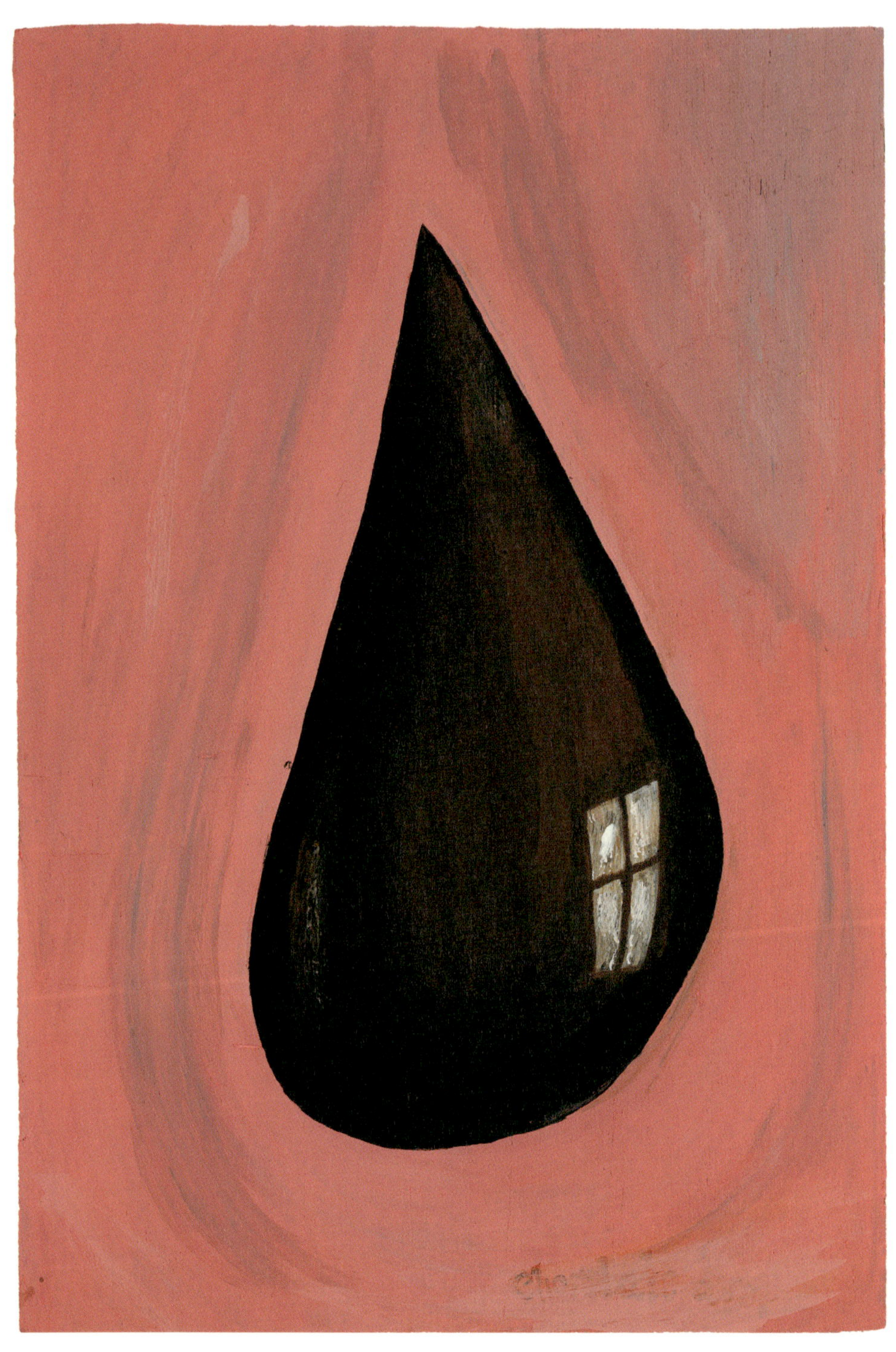

60

Chocolate Drop

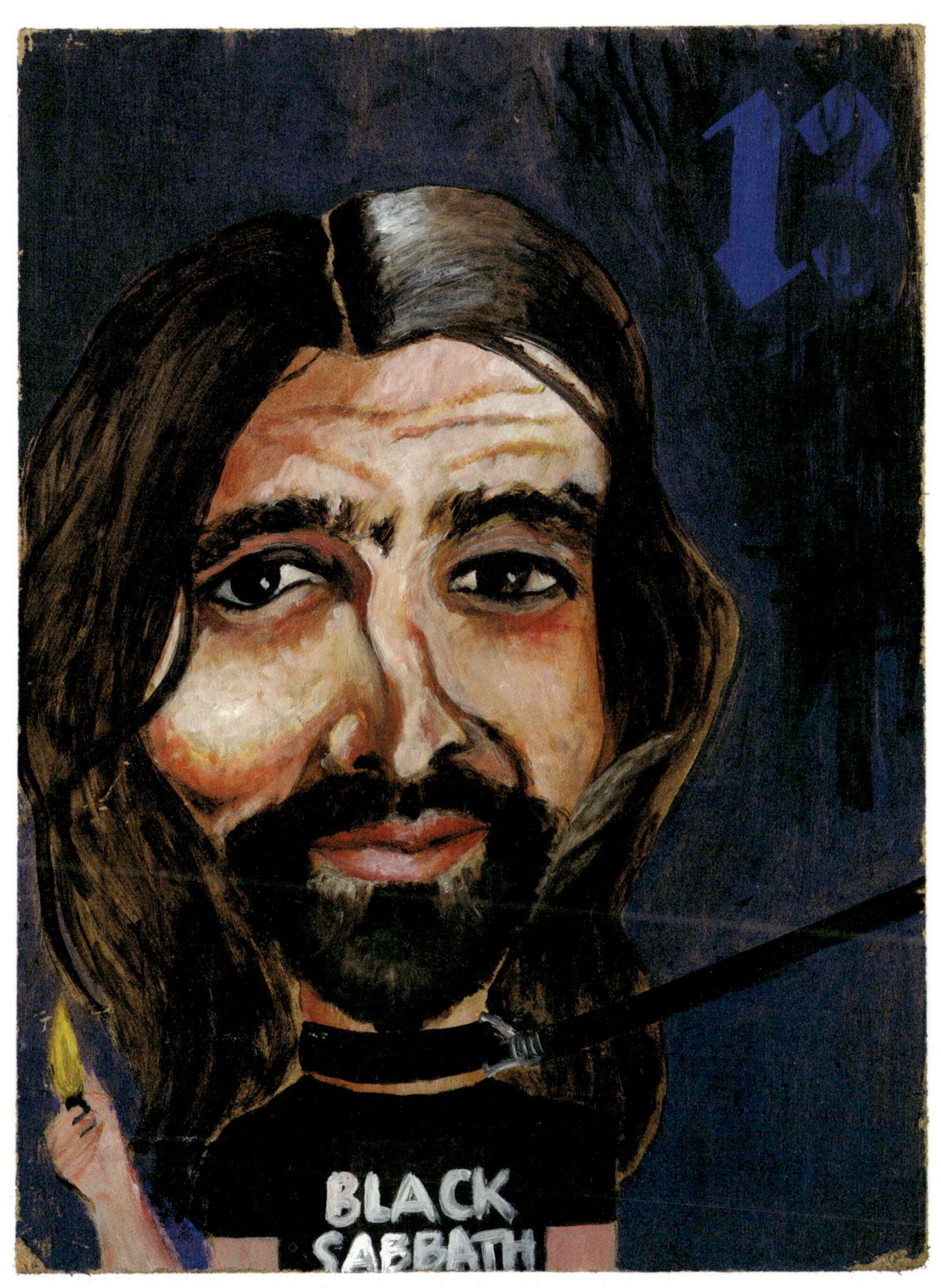

Stranger

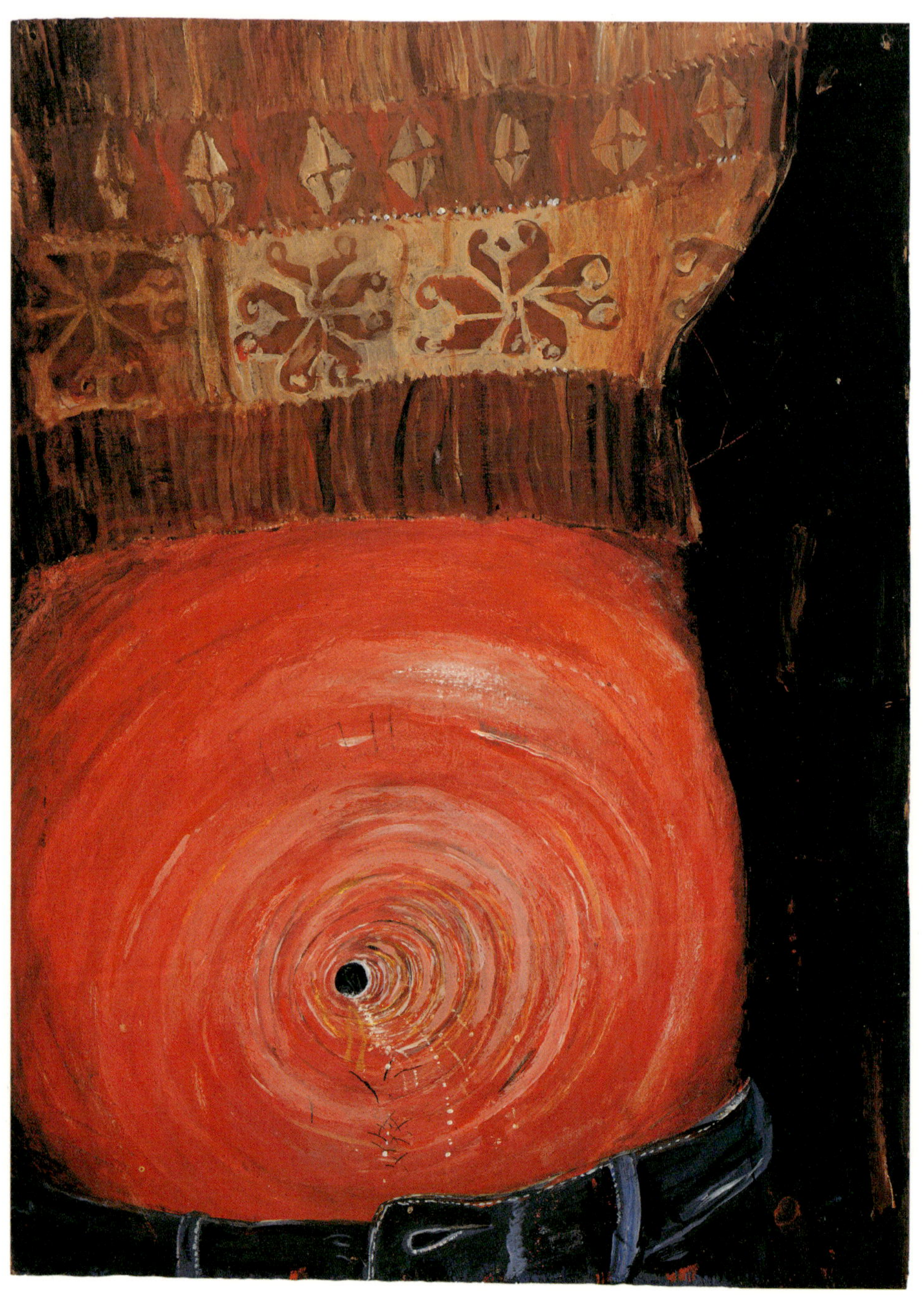

Belly-Button Whirlpool

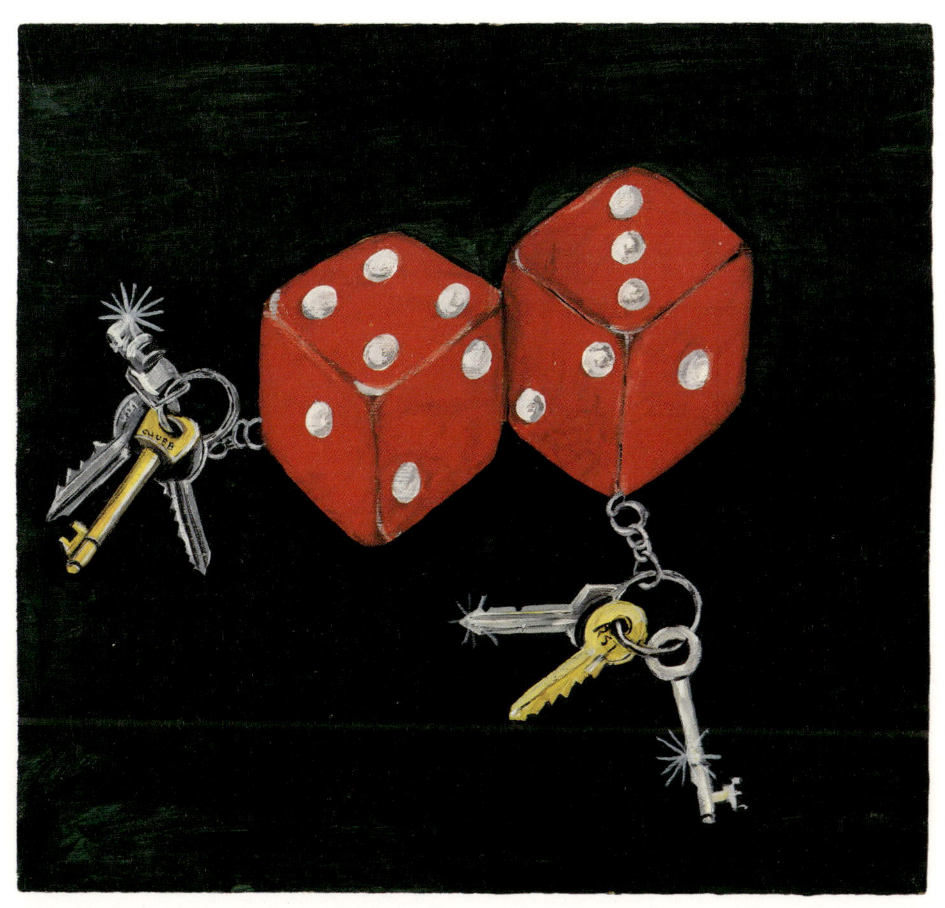

Keys in a Basket

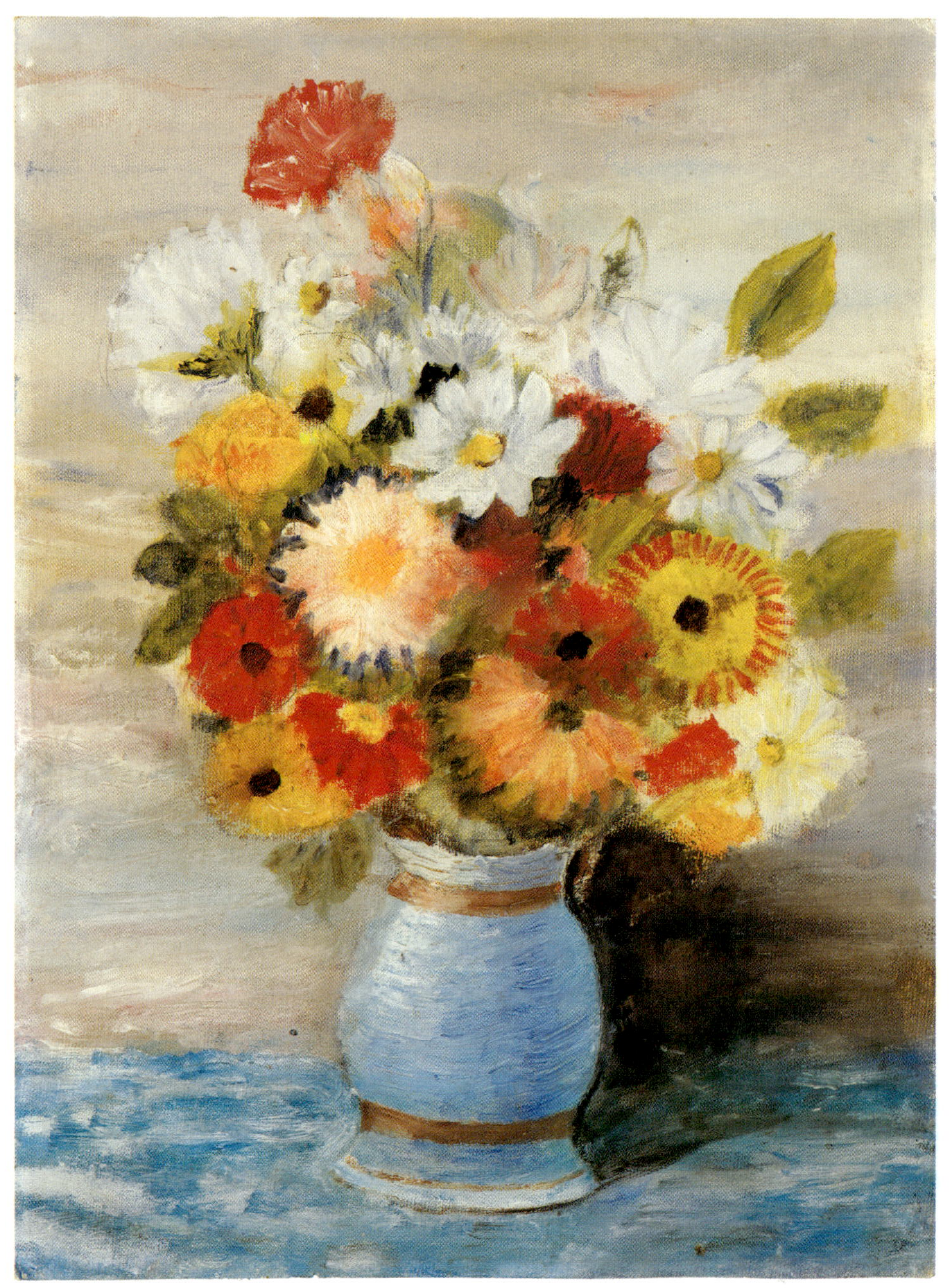

Flowers

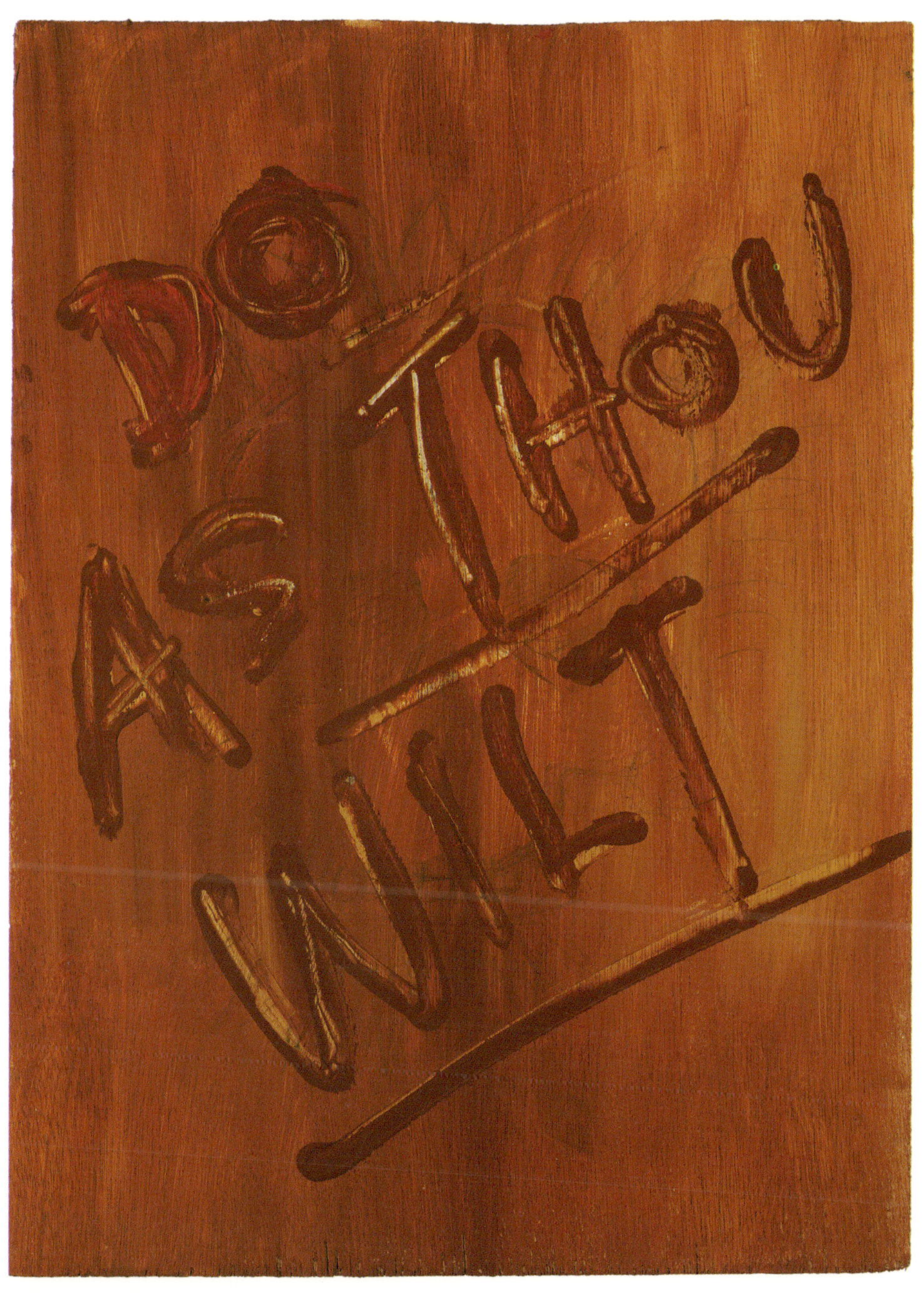

Do As Thou Wilt

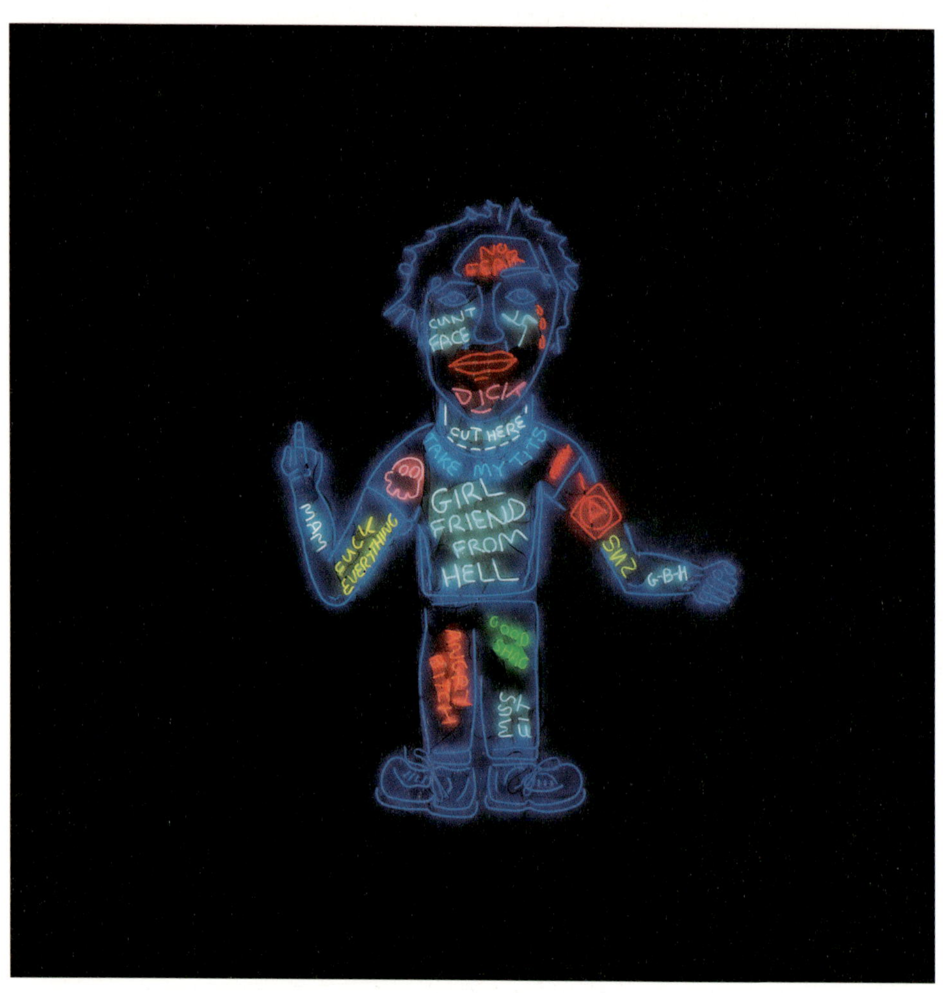

Puny Undernourished Kid & Girlfriend From Hell (Diptych), 2004

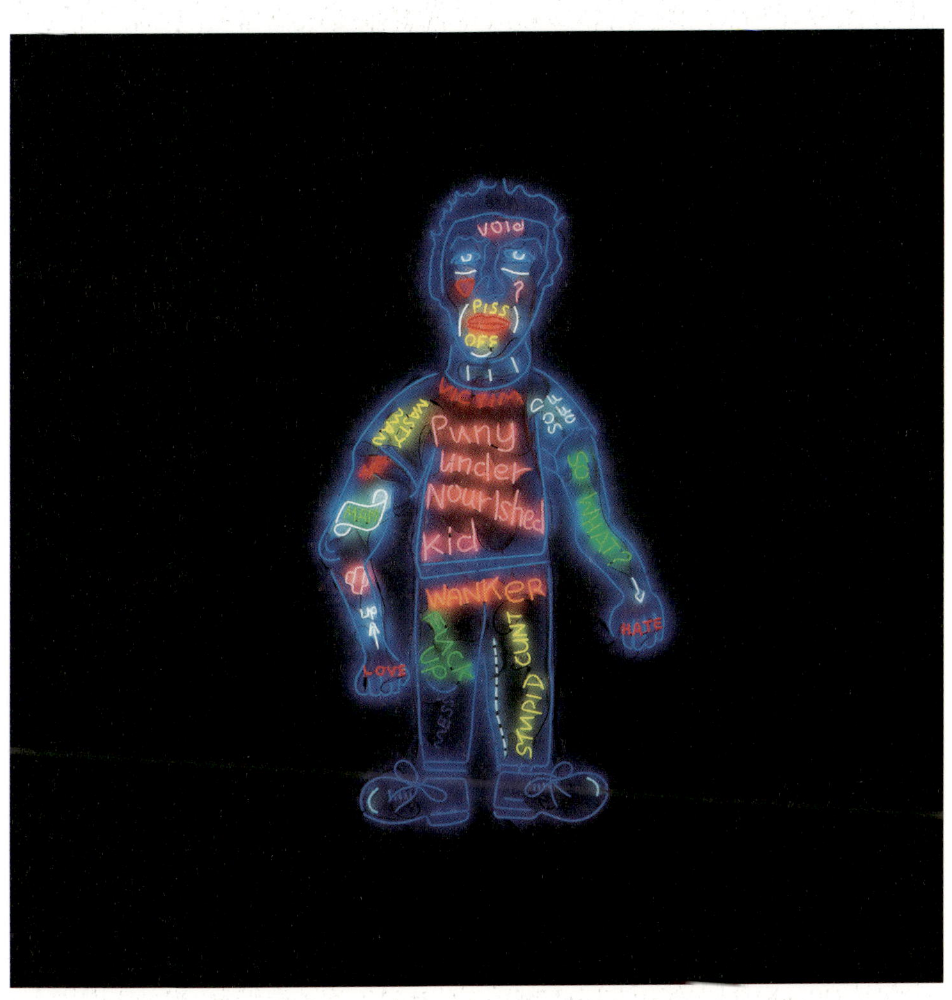

VOID
?
PISS OFF
VICTIM
Puny under Nourished kid
SO WHAT?
MAD
WANKER
STUPID CUNT
UP
LOVE
HATE

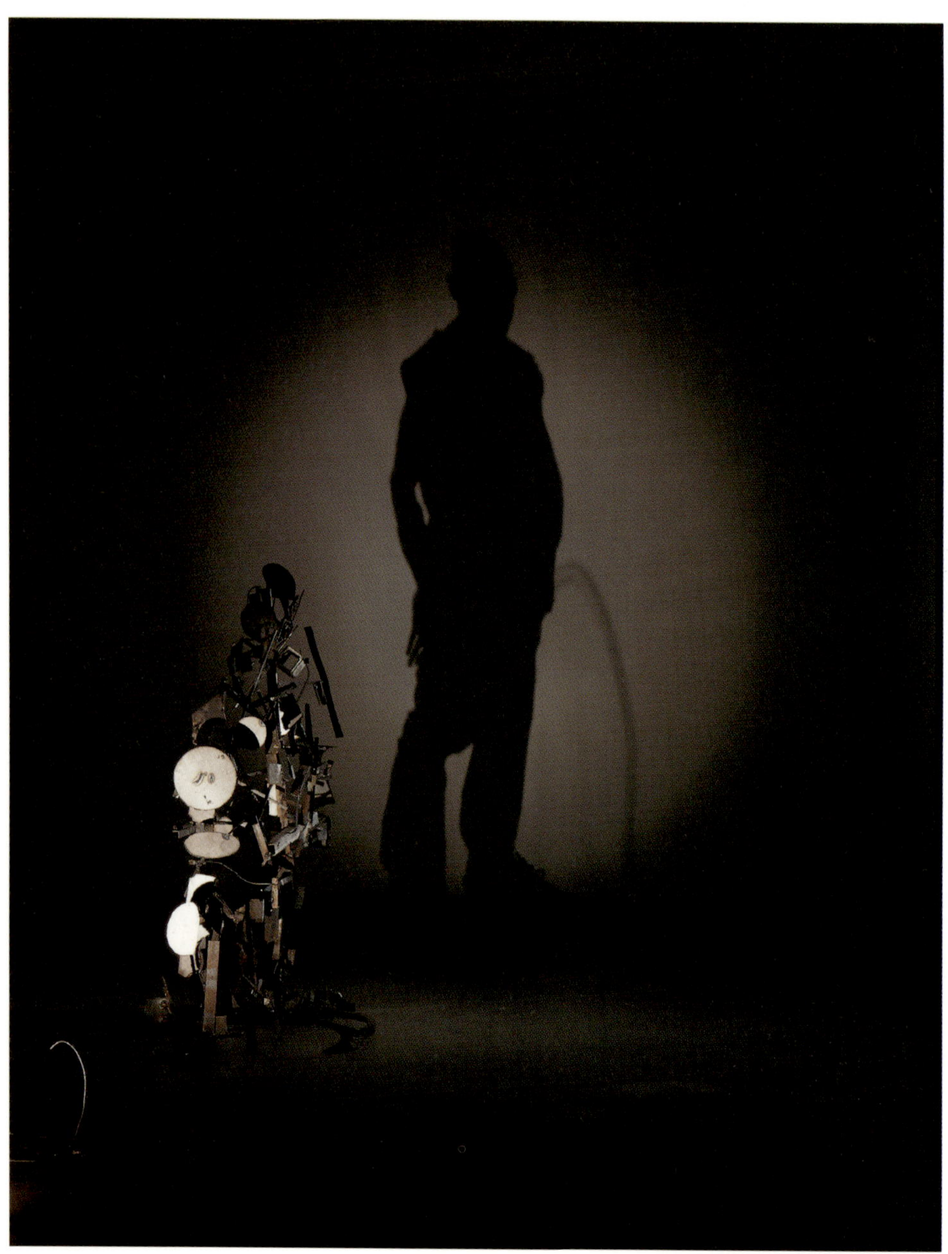

HE/SHE (Diptych), 2004

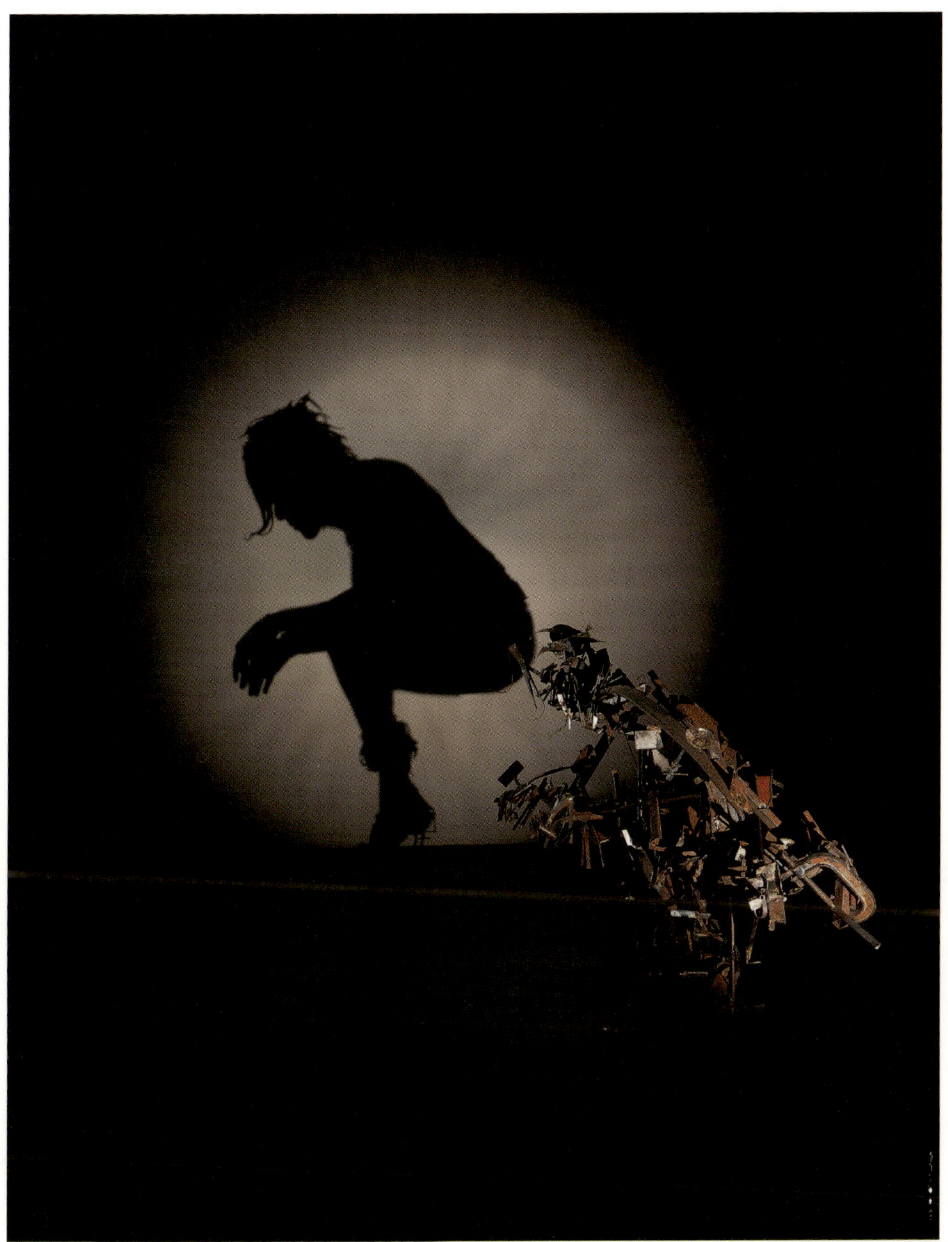

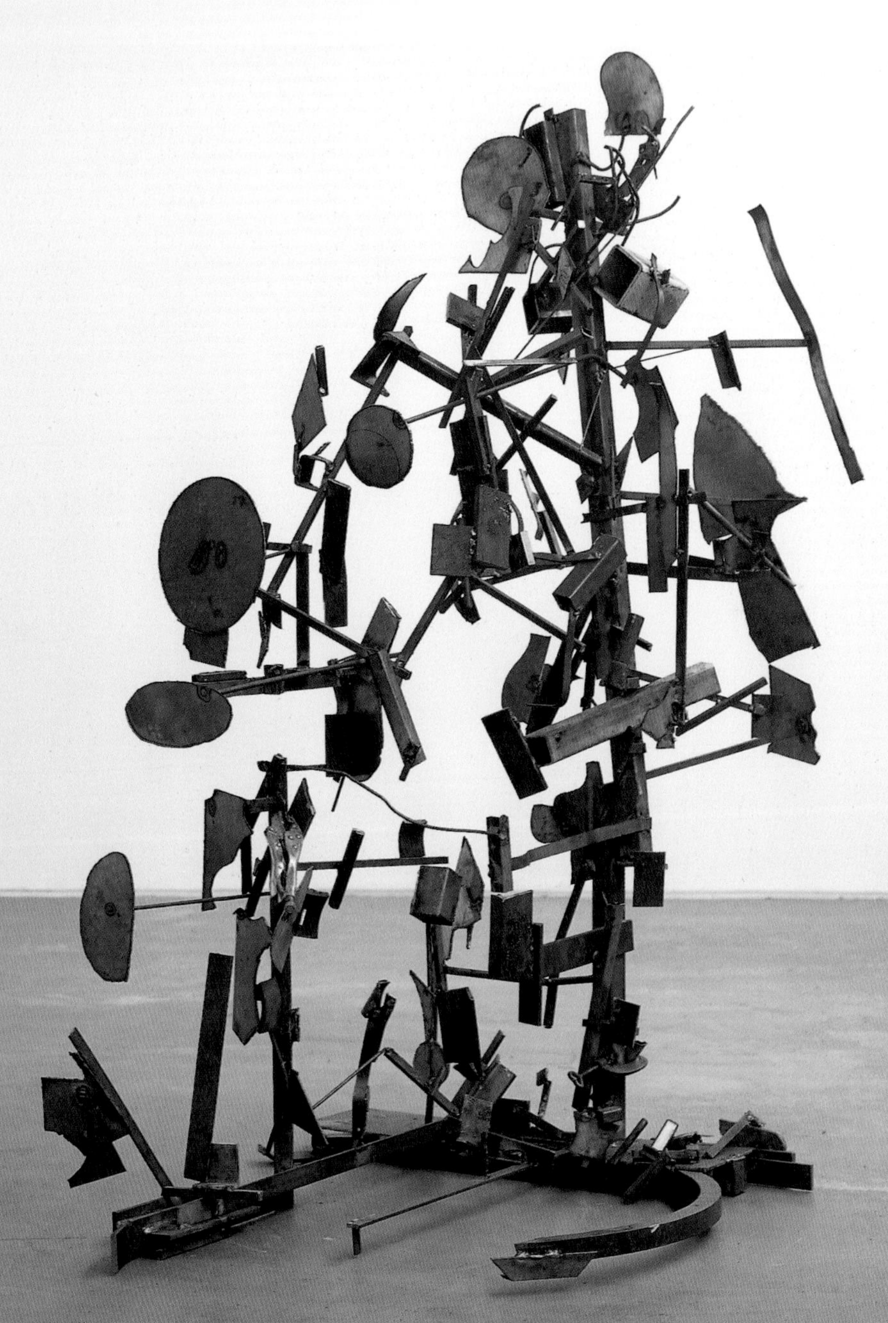

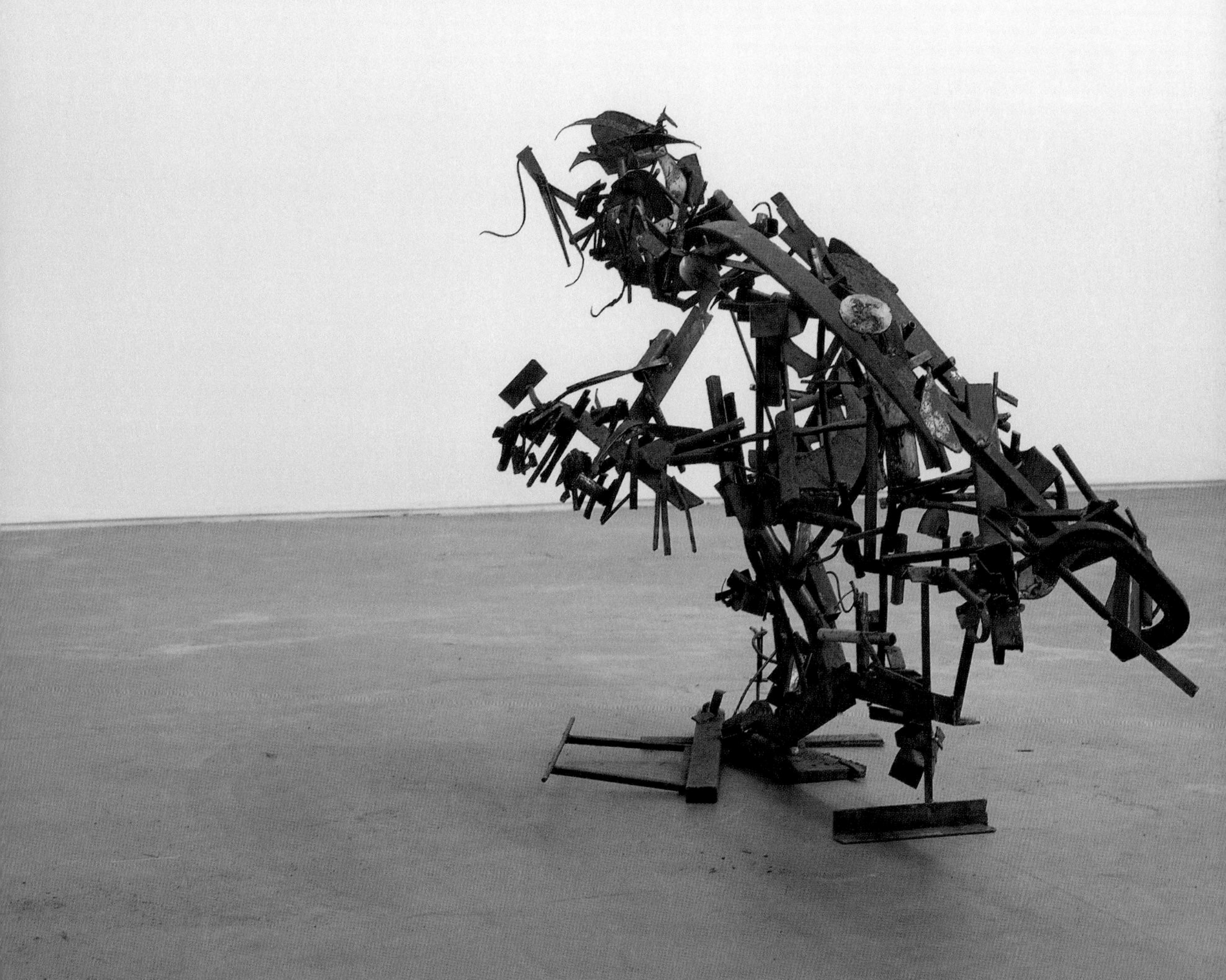

Untitled (Spinning Heads), 2005

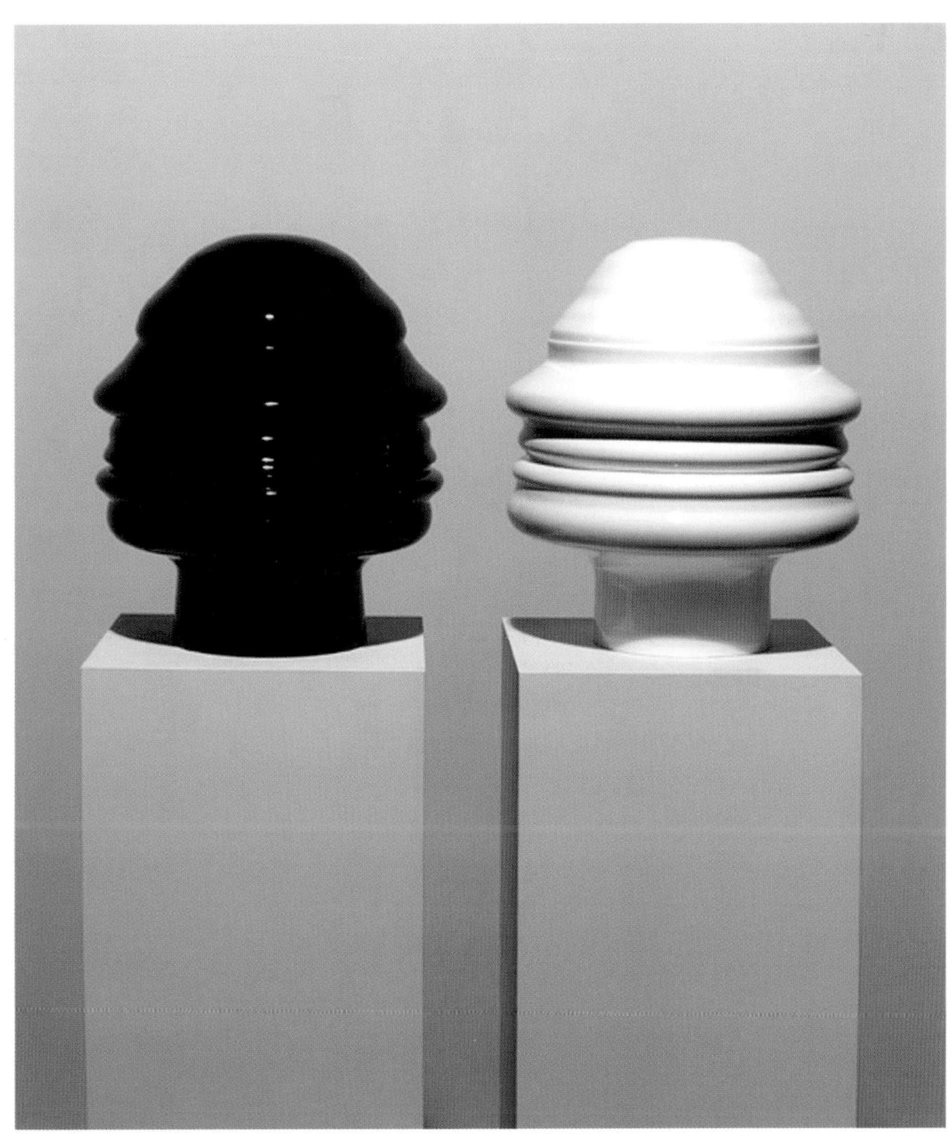

The Joy of Sex, 2005

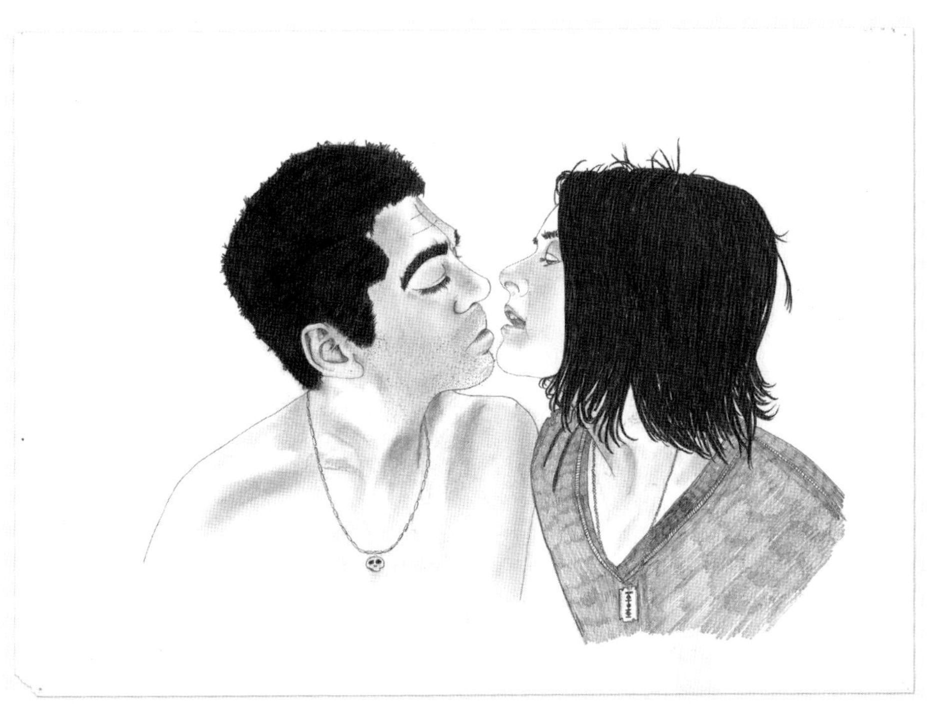

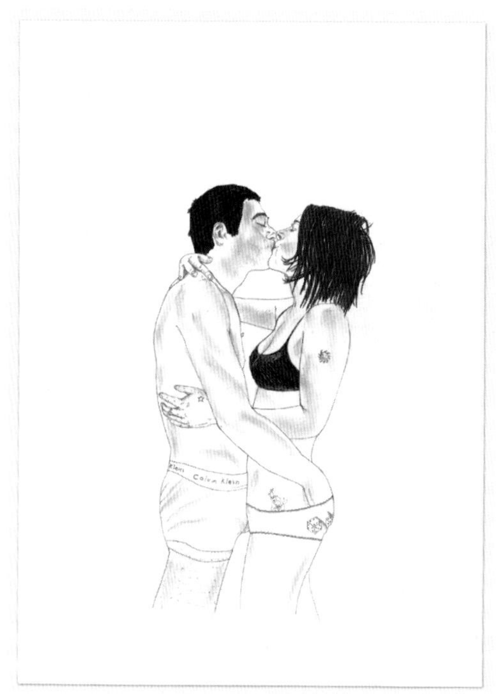

Hands down Pants

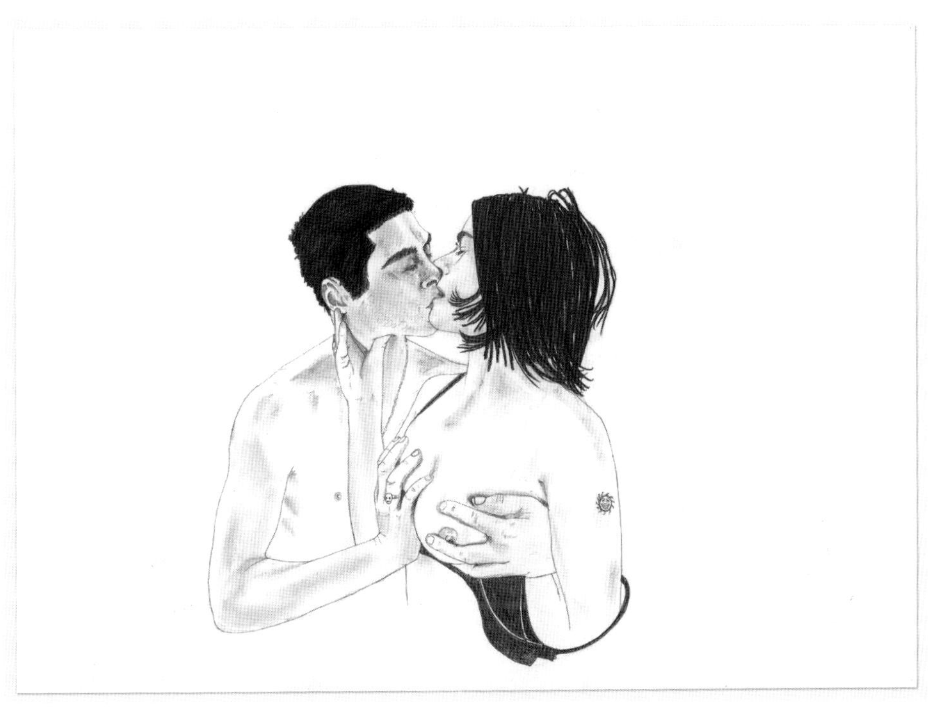

No Bra

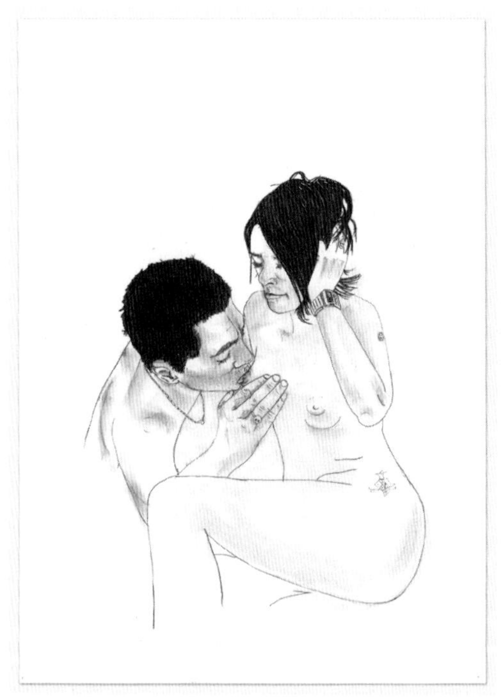

Pretty to the Point

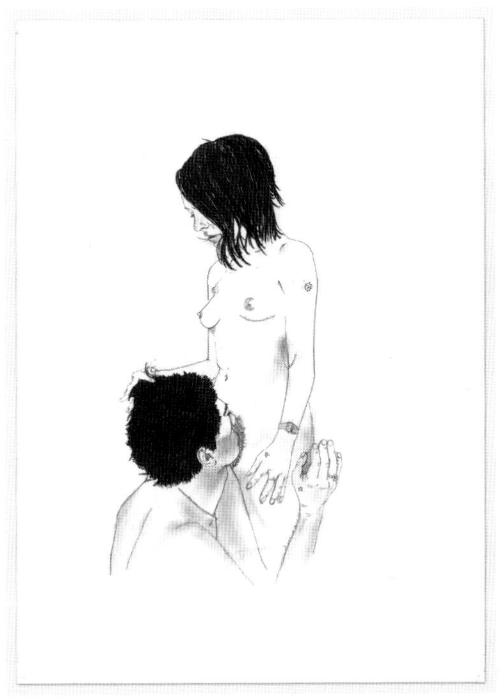

Juicy Peaches

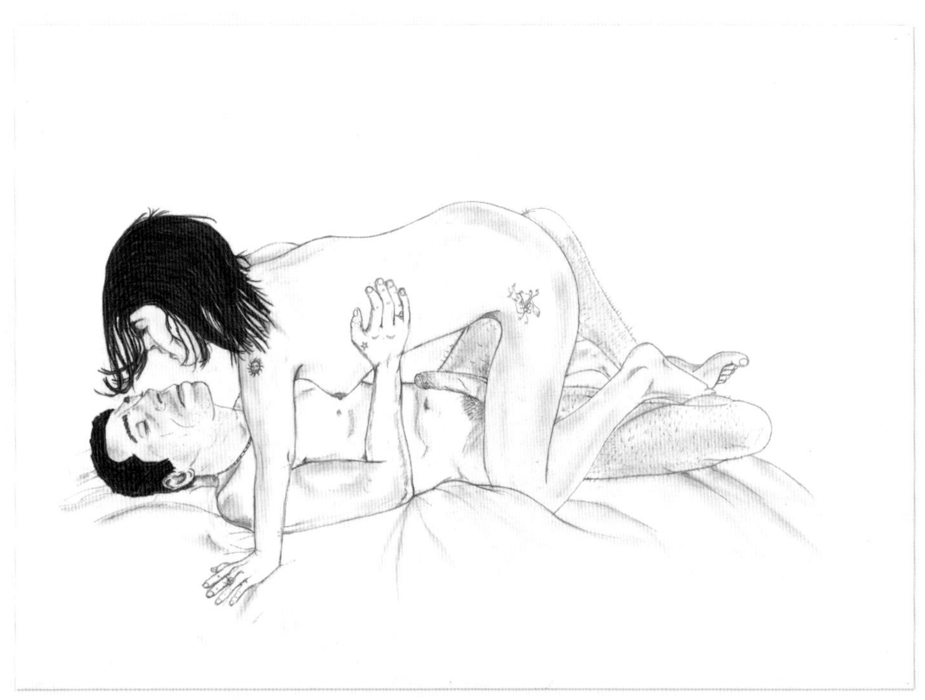

Back to the Front

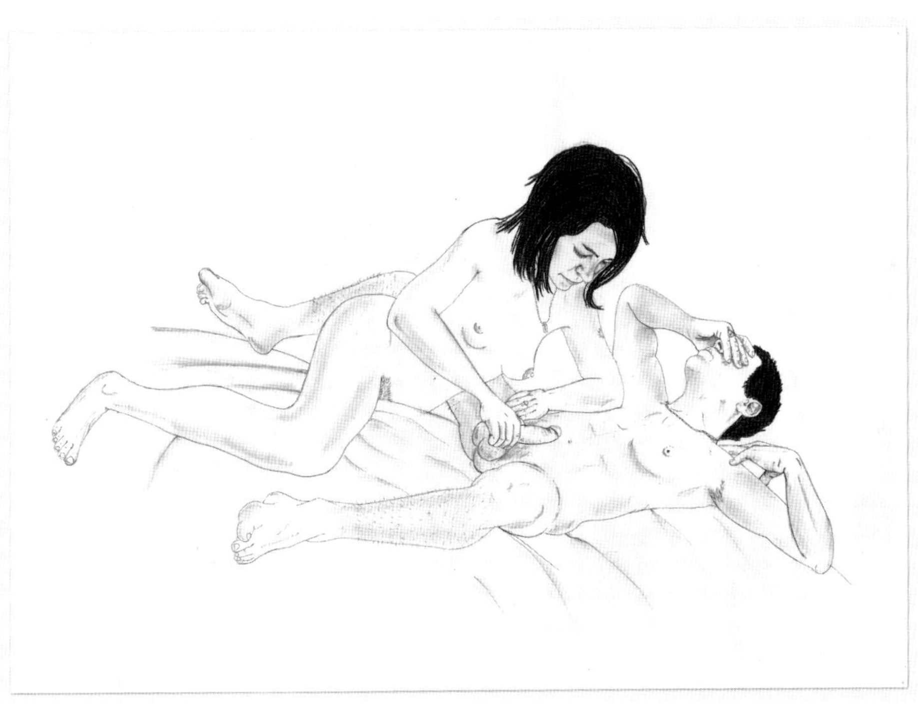

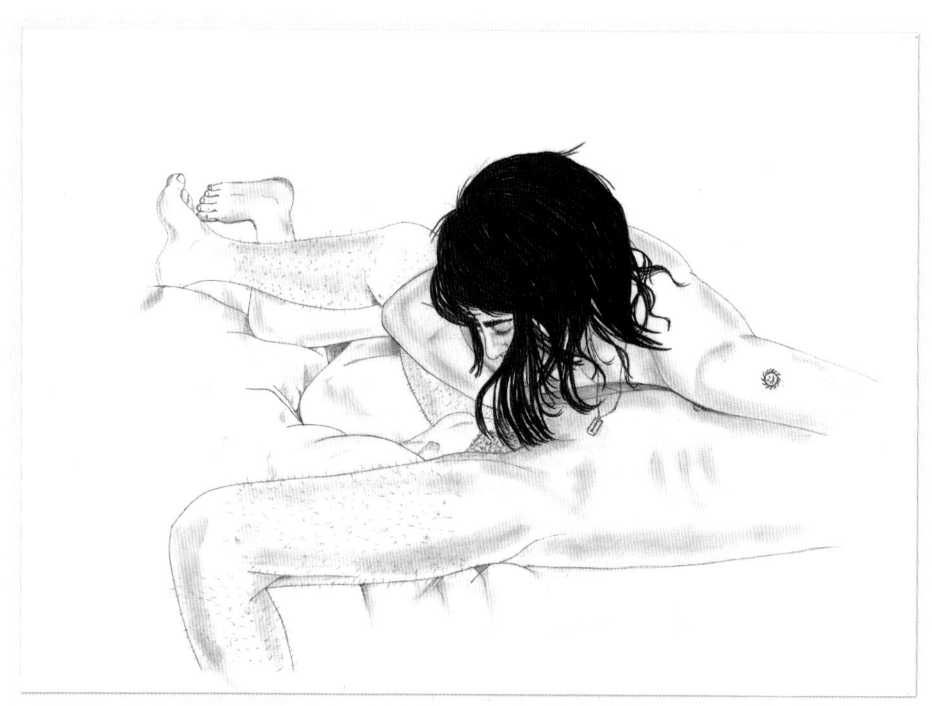

Mouth Fuck

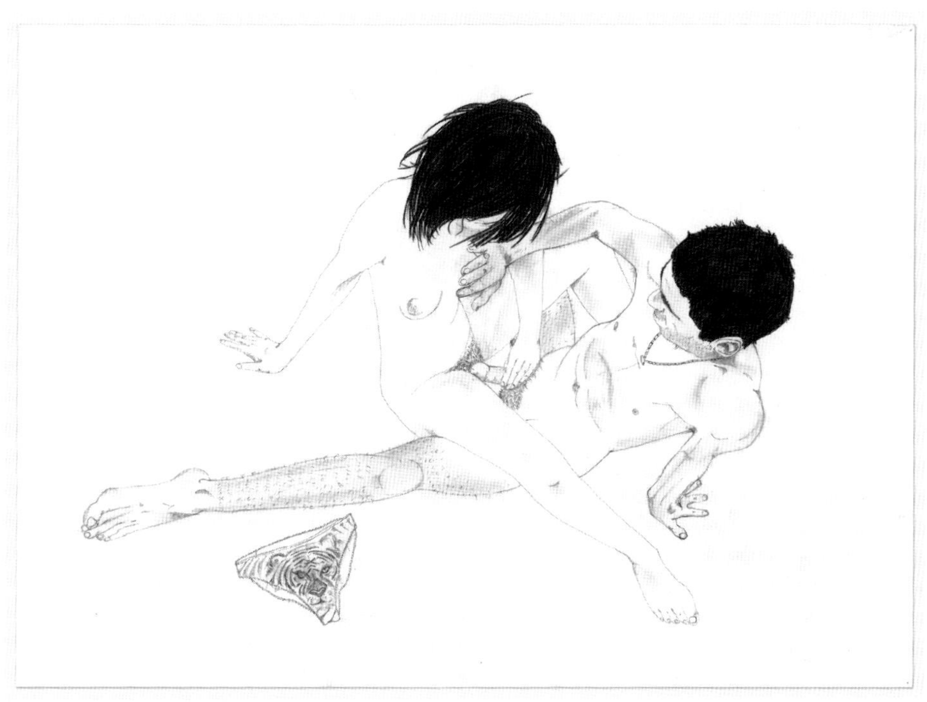

Easy Tiger

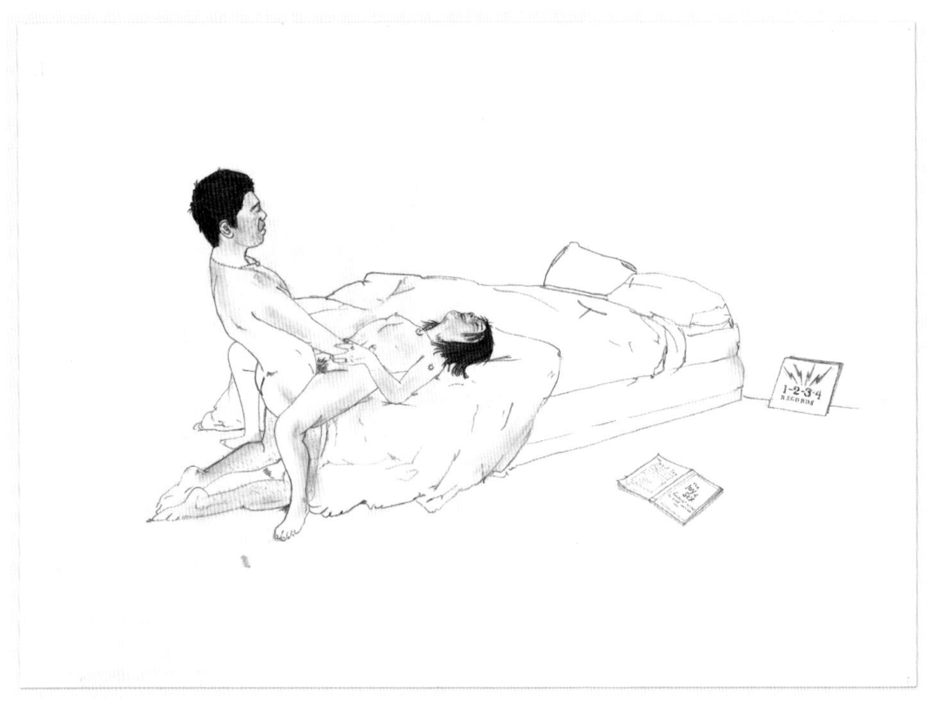

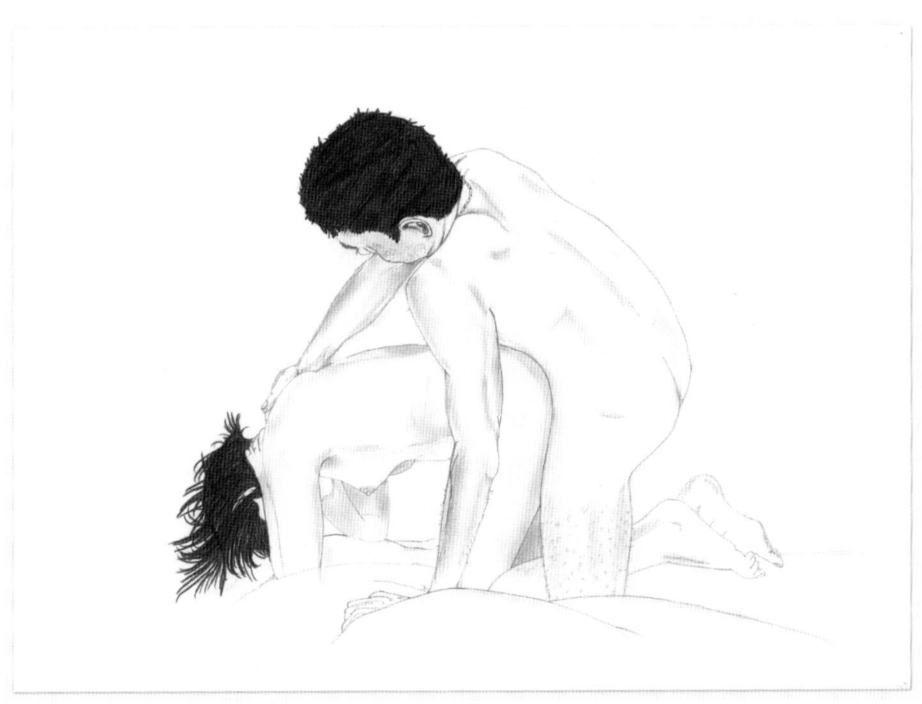

Violent Bliss

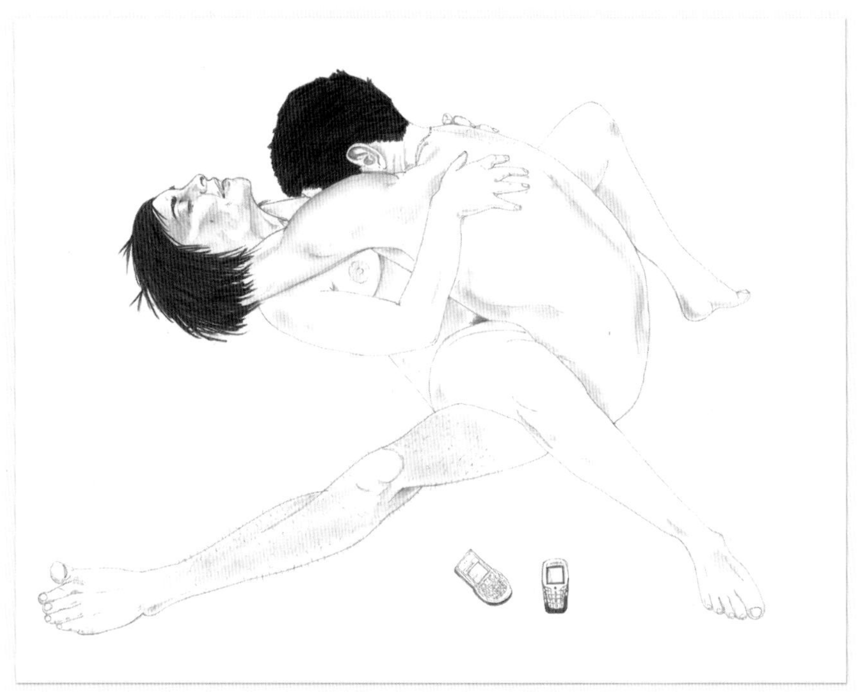

Phone Sex

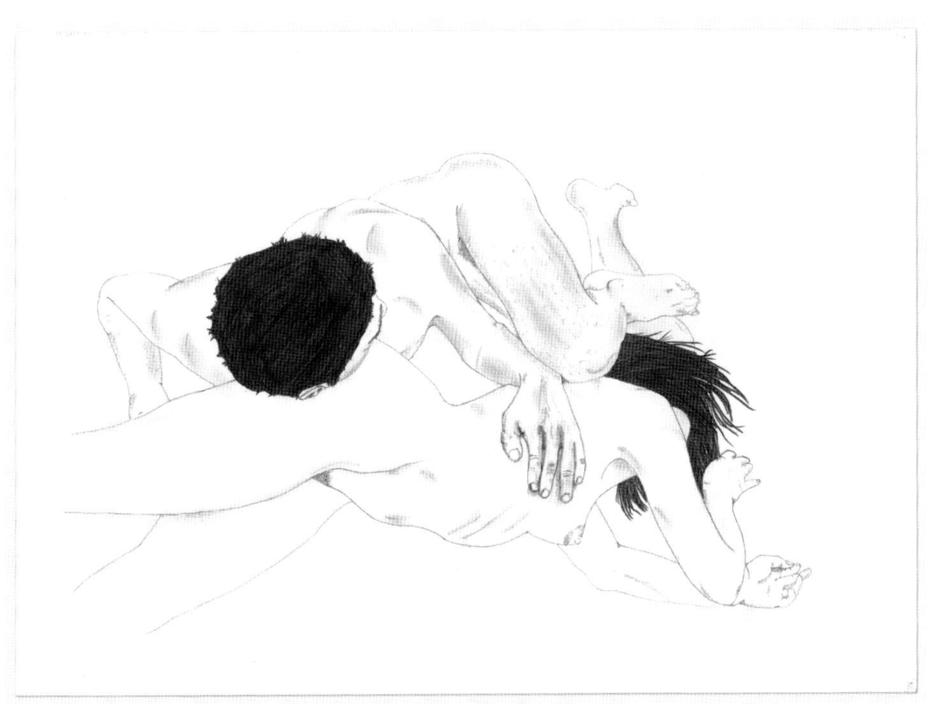

Simply Natural

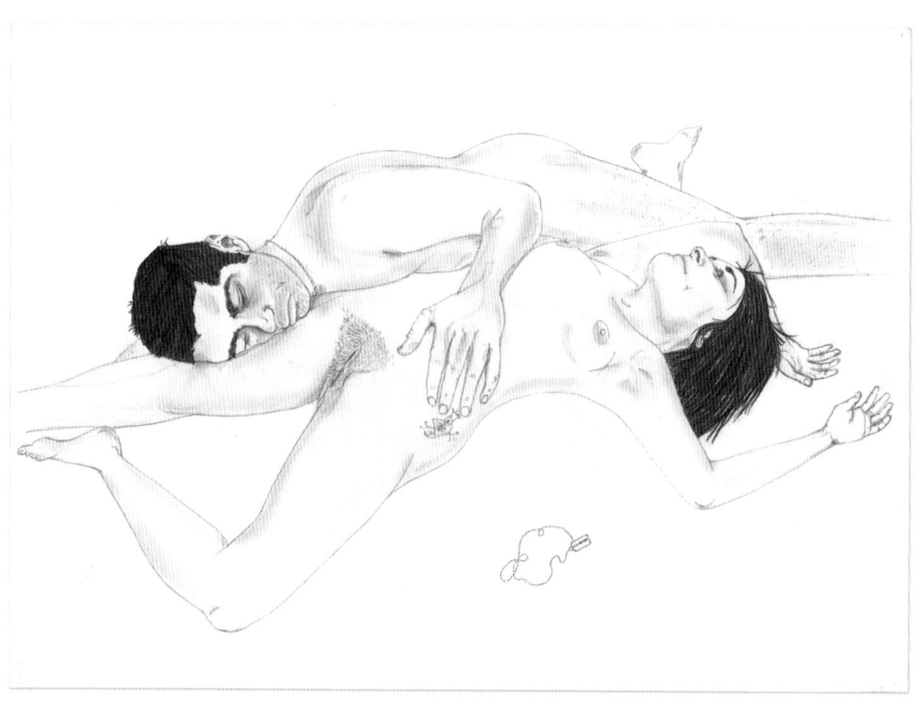

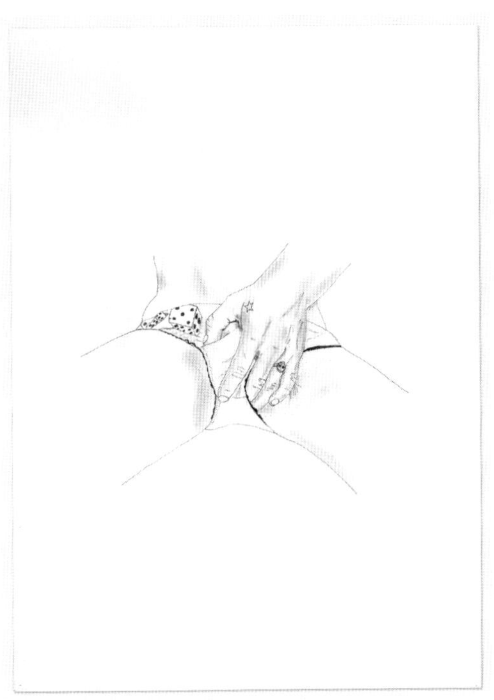

Lucky Dip

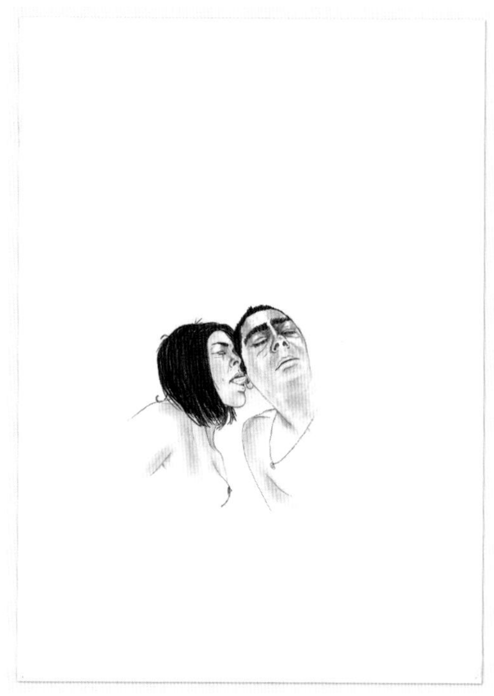

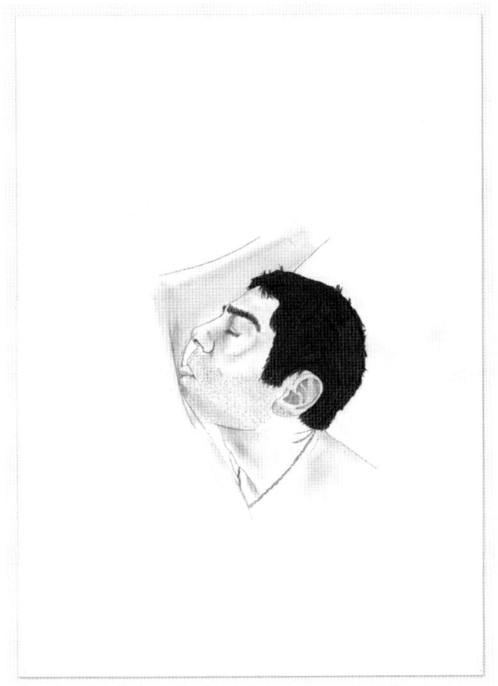

Pure Trouble

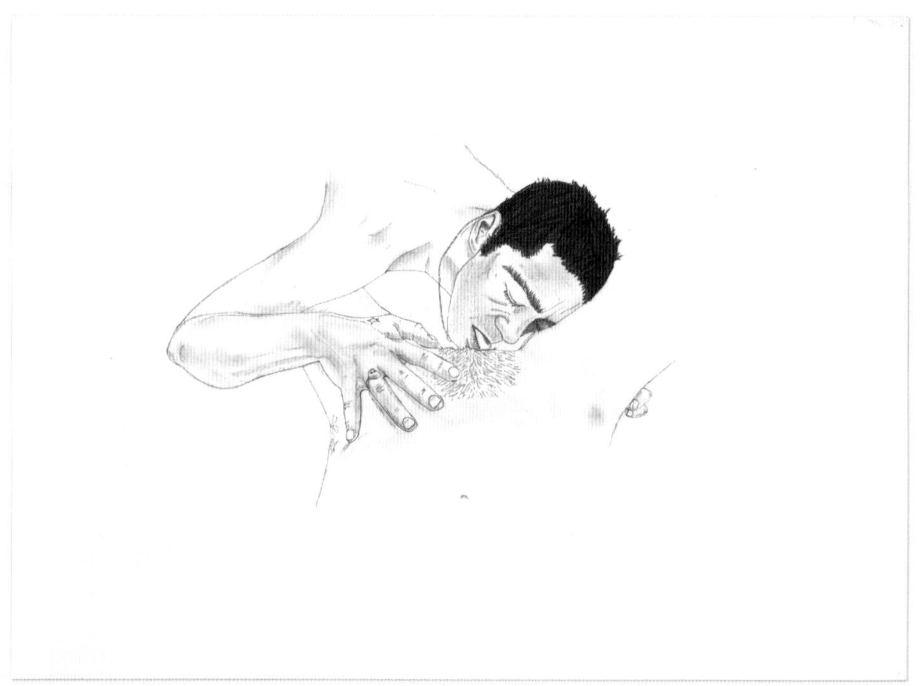

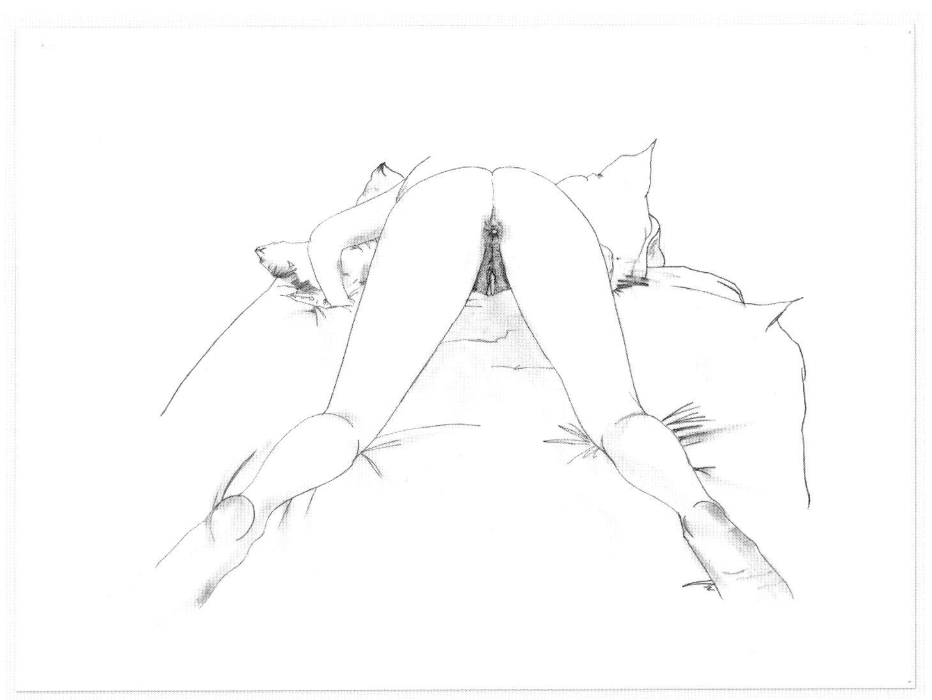

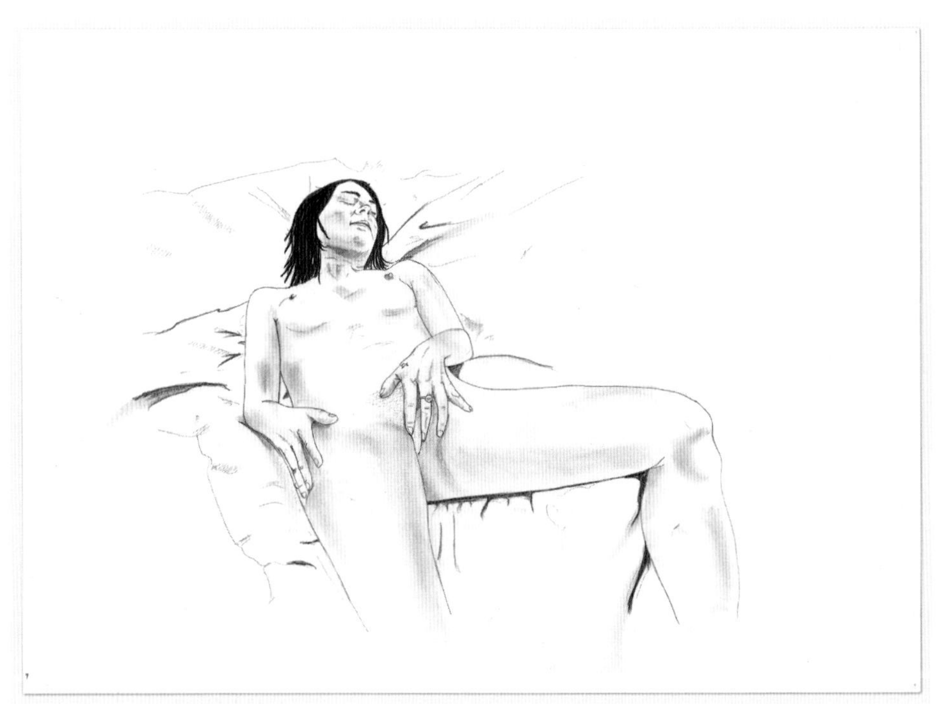

Selfish Cunt

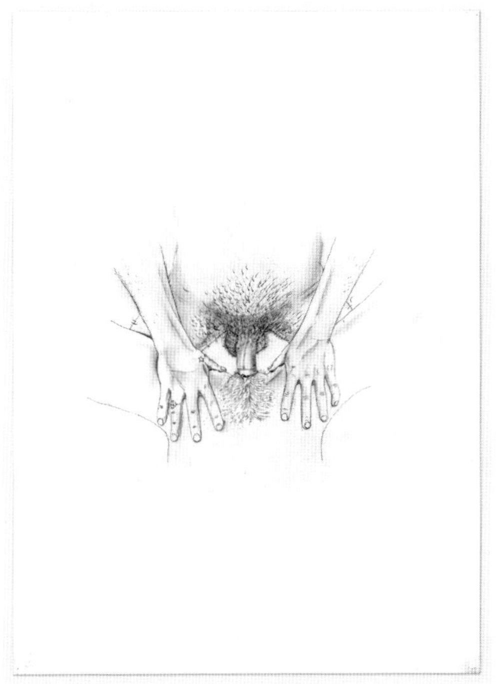

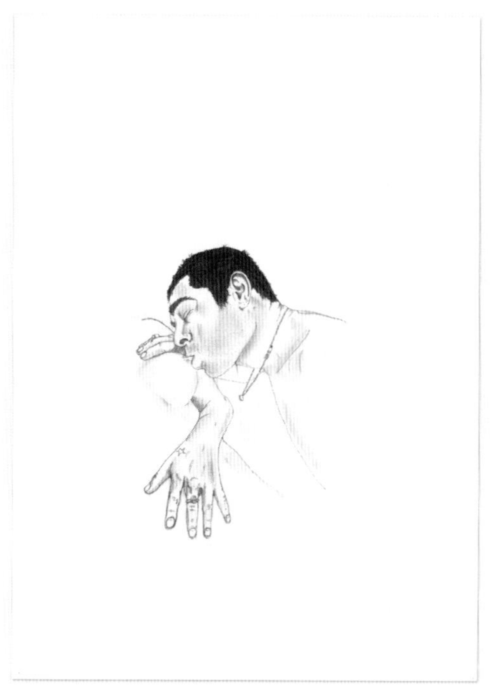

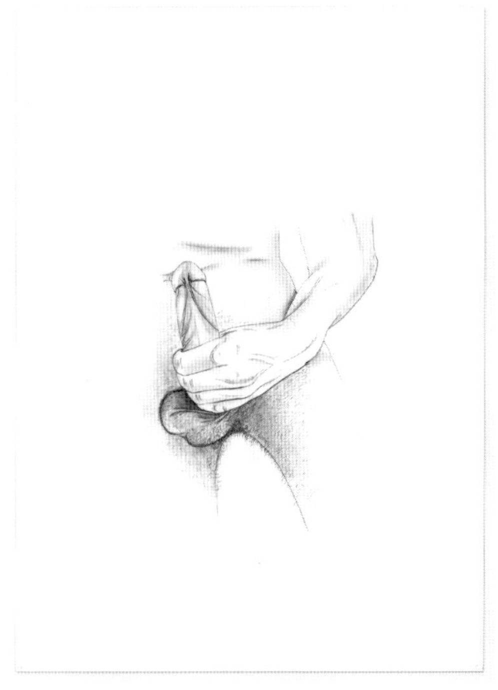

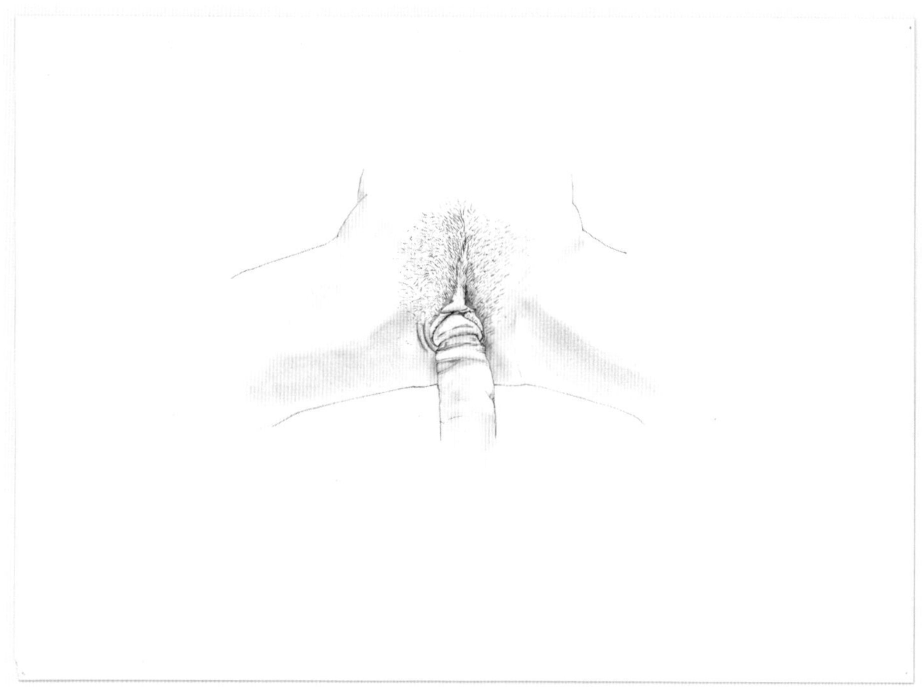

Enter the Dragon

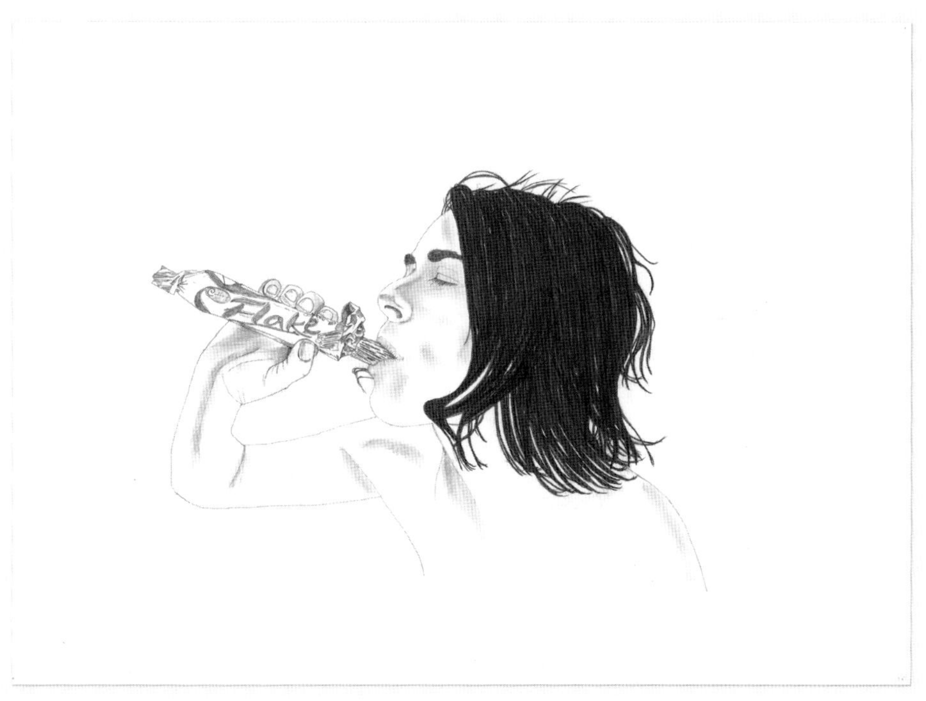

Chocolate Dip

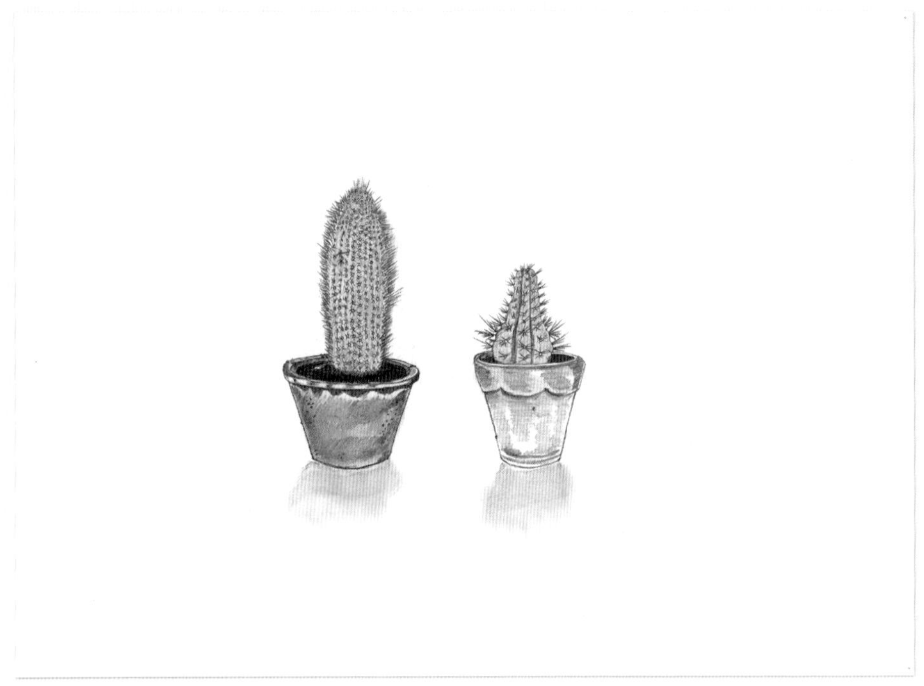

Twin Peaks

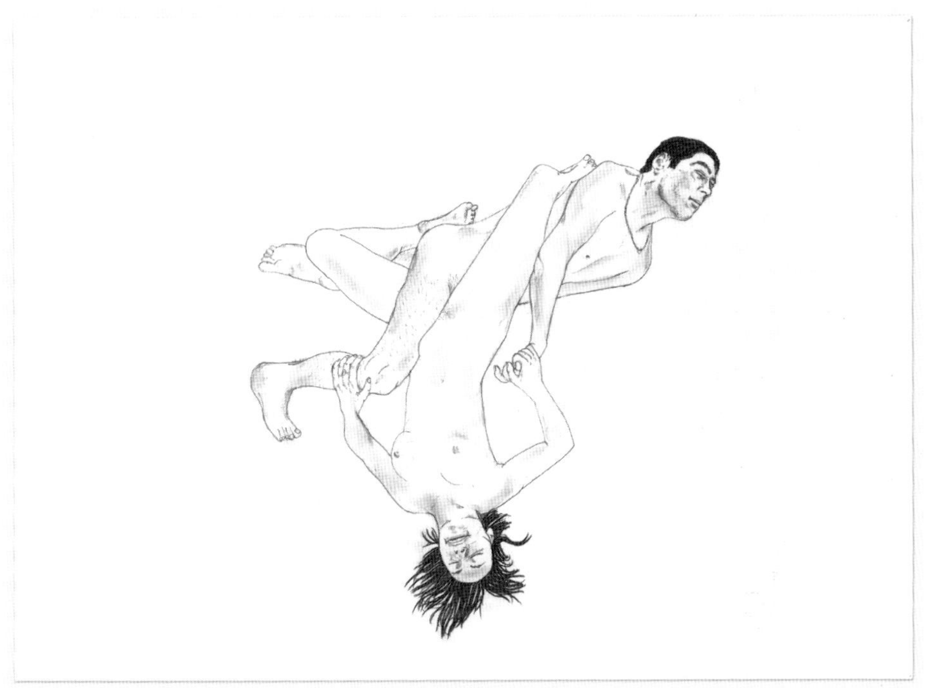

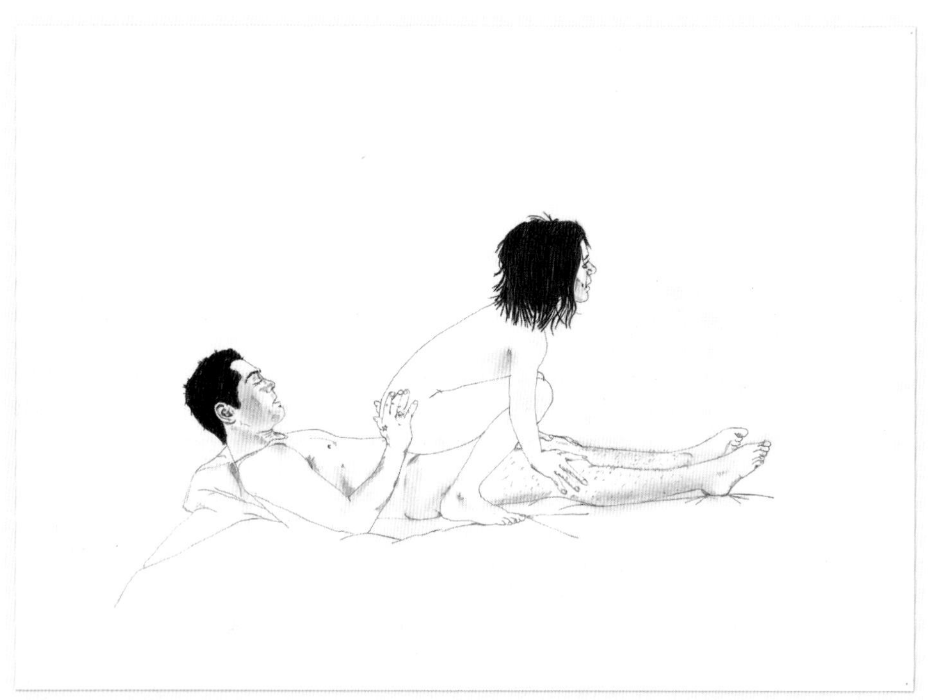

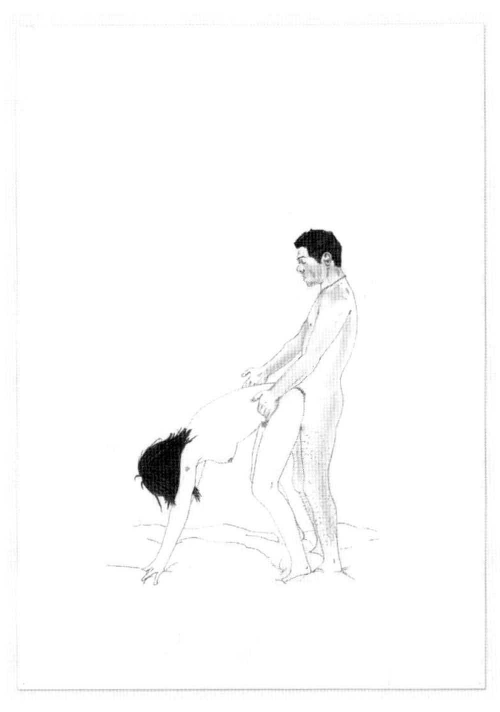

103

Buttfuck

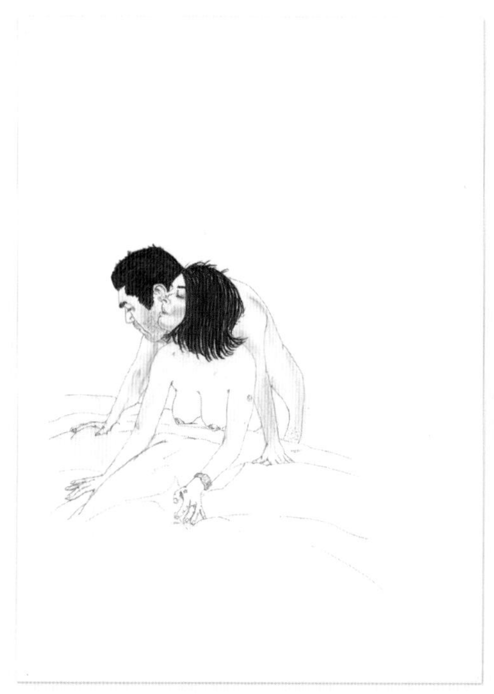

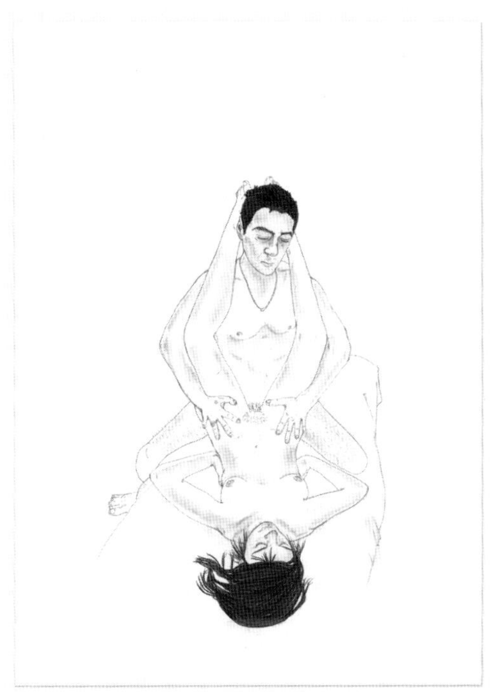

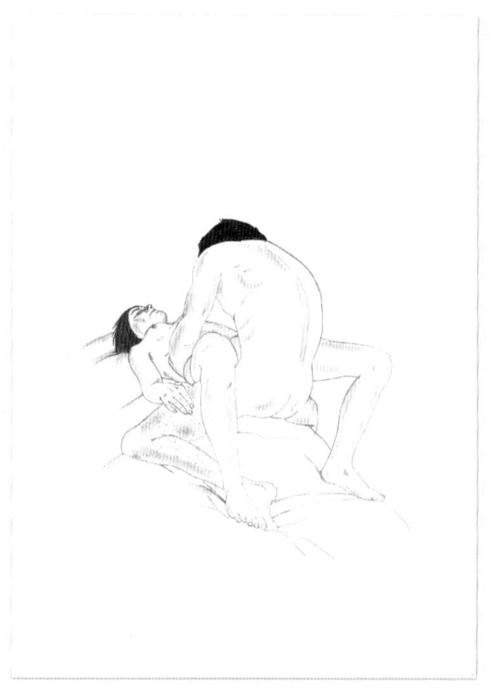

106

Pumping

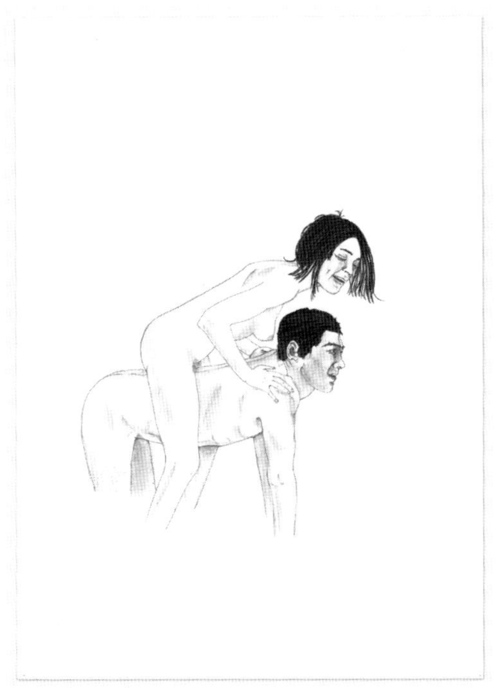

Horseplay

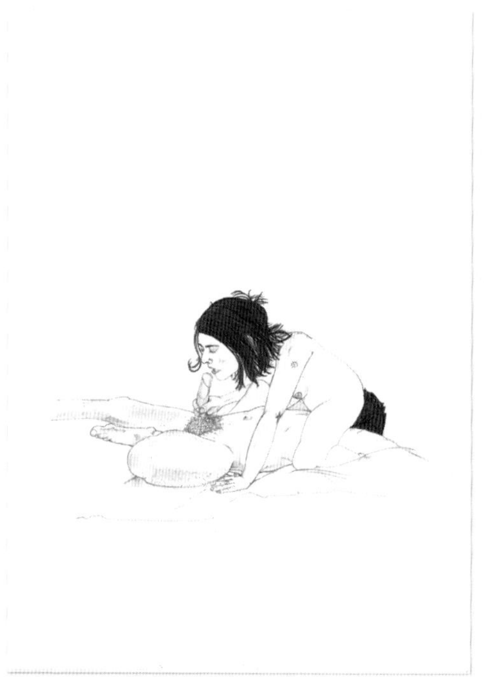

The 69 Club

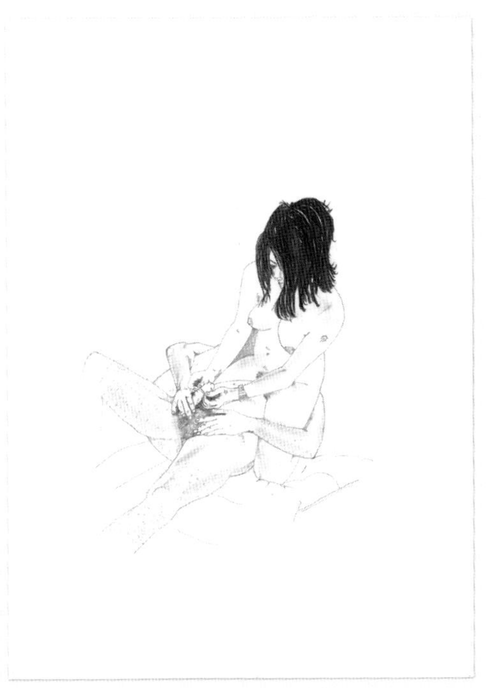

The Safer Sex

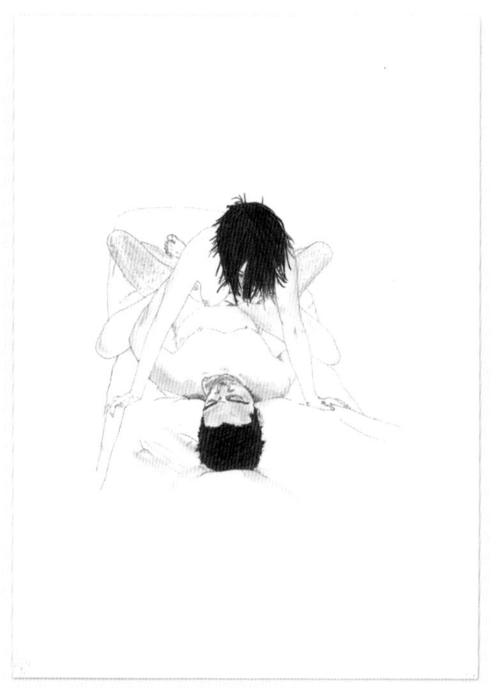

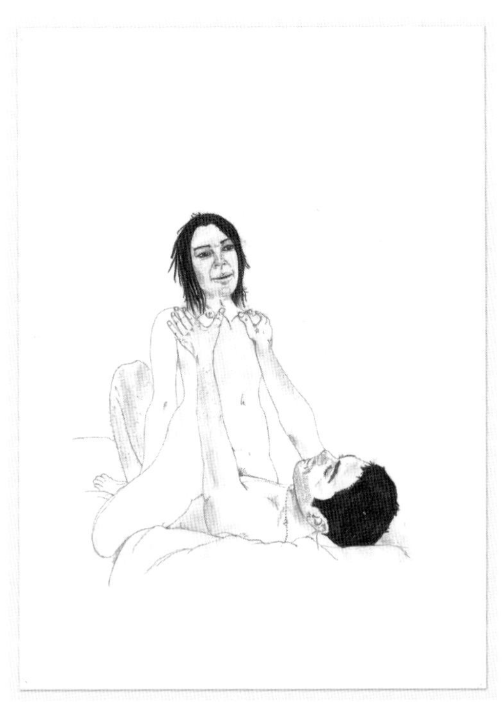

Nipple Reaction

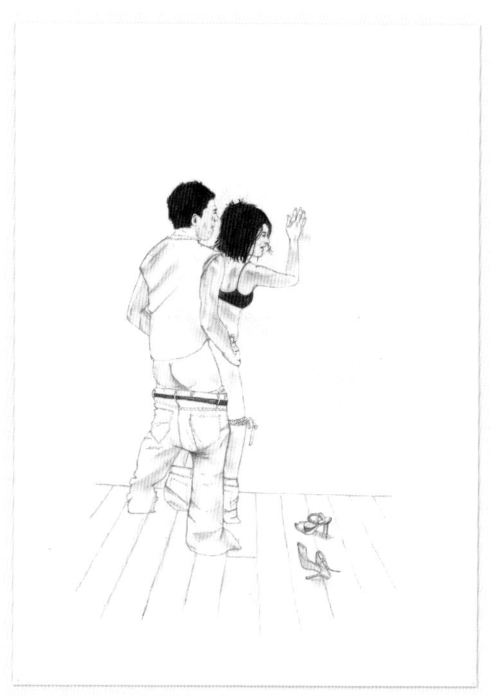

Fast Fuck

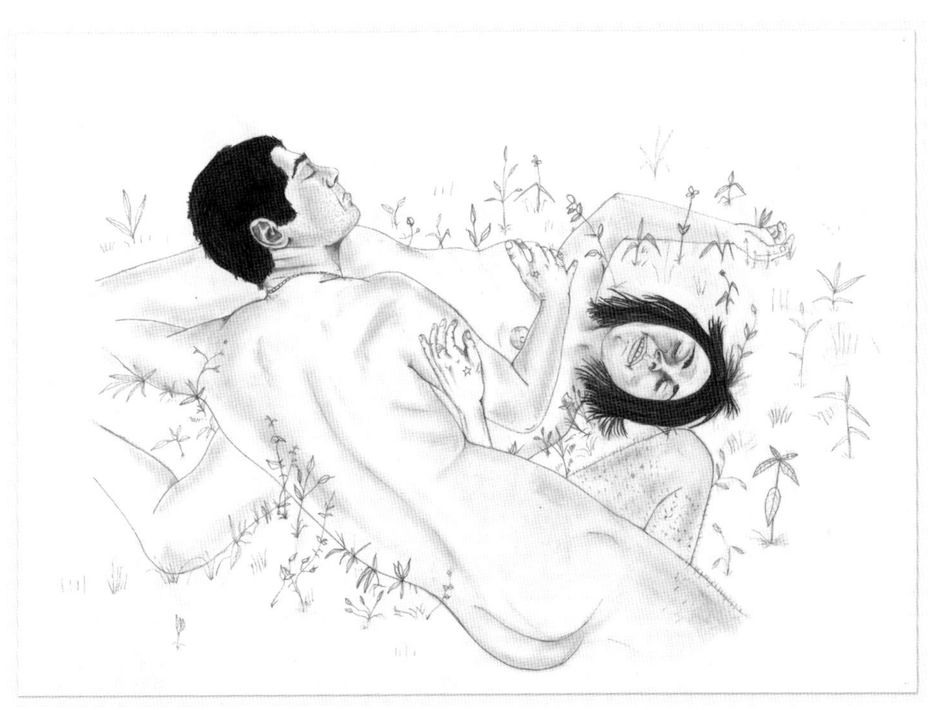

113

Wildlife

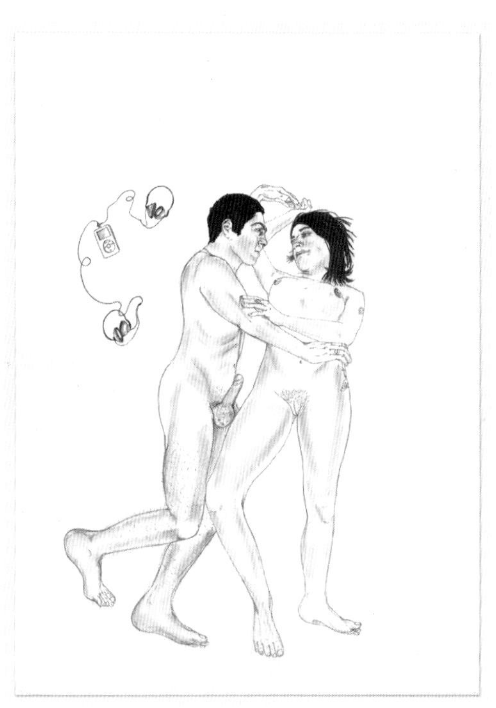

Black Narcissus, 2006

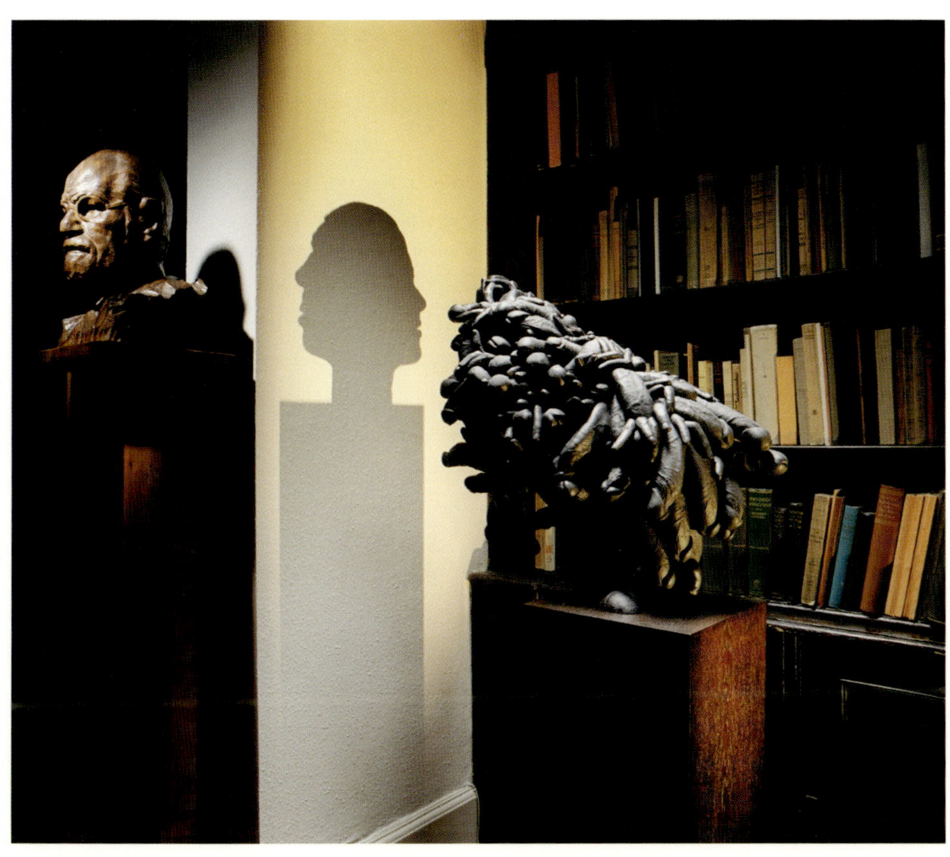

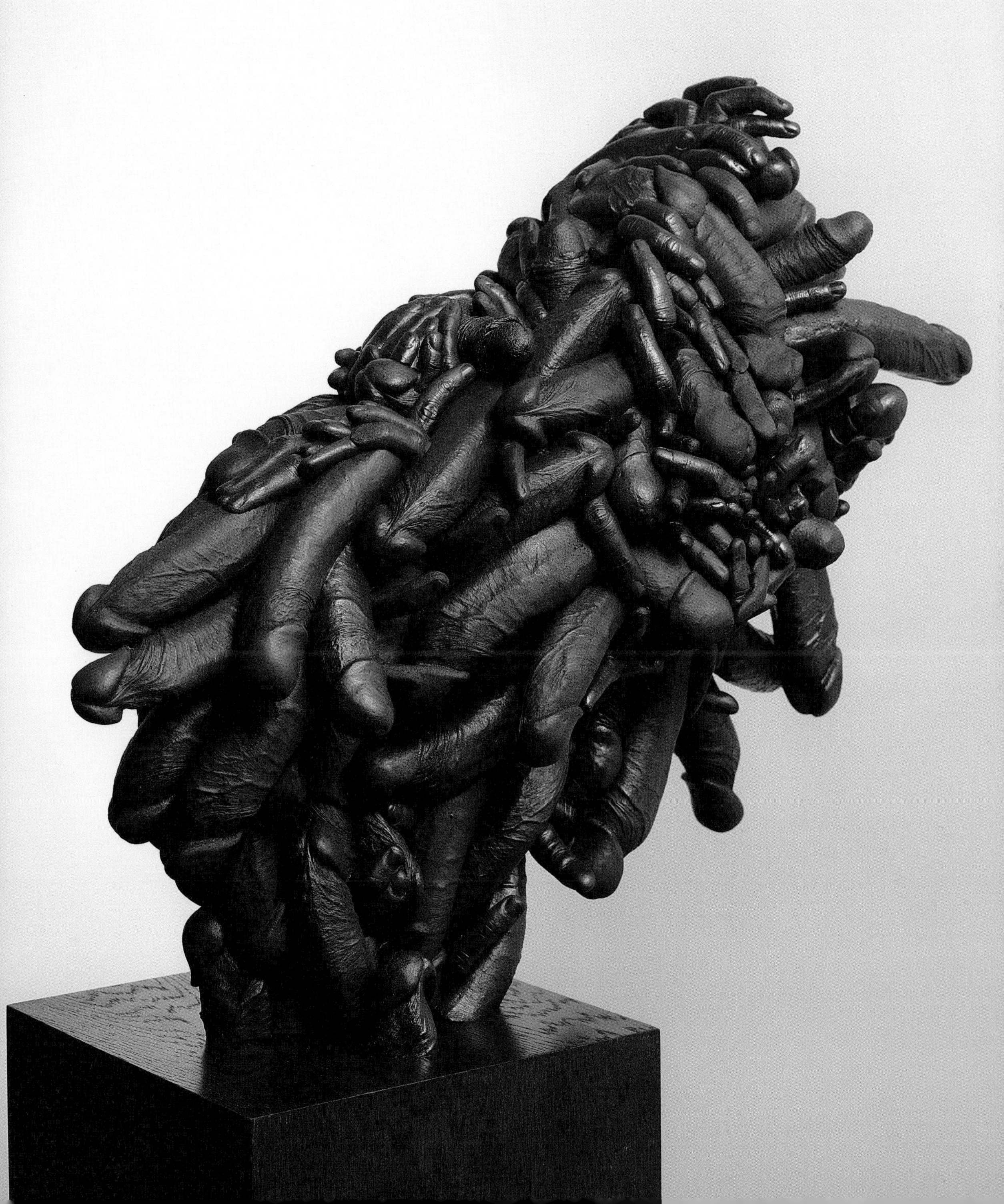

fuckingbeautiful (hot pink version, detail), 2008

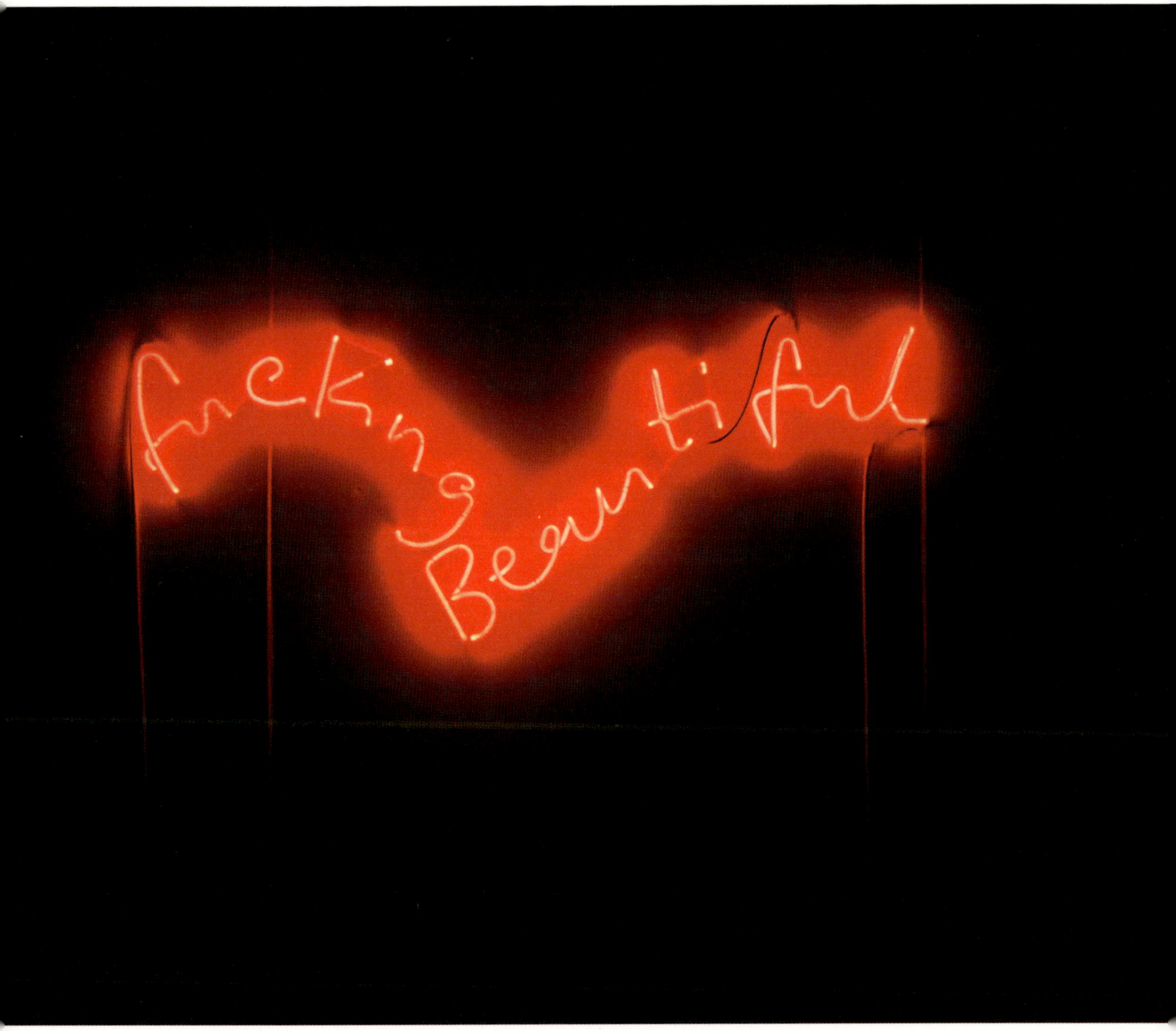

fucking
Beautiful

LIST OF WORKS

50 Ways to Leave Your Lover, 1996
49 illustrations, ink on paper
Dimensions variable; 113 x 113 x 3 cm, framed

Excessive Sensual Indulgence, 1996
312 colored UFO reflector caps, lamps, and holders,
Foamex, PVC film, spray paint, and electronic light
sequencer (4-channel bubble & chase effect)
187 x 88 x 7 cm
Edition of 3/3 + 2 AP

Forever, 1996
196 ice-white UFO reflector caps, lamps, and holders,
Foamex, and electronic light sequencer (3-channel
shimmer effect)
76.5 x 232.5 x 7 cm
Edition of 5 + 2 AP + 2/2 AC + 1 HC

London Swings (poster), 1997
Photomontage on poster
70 x 84 cm, framed
Edition of 2 unique versions

Dirty White Trash (with Gulls), 1998
Six months' worth of artists' trash, two taxidermy
seagulls, and light projector
Dimensions variable

Simply Natural, 1999
Photographic montage on hair-dye boxes
Two parts: 14.5 x 9 x 6 cm each
Edition of 10/10 + 3 AP

*From F**k to Trash*, 2000
Acrylic on medium-density fiberboard
122 x 122 cm

Masters of the Universe, 2000
Translucent resin, fiberglass, and human hair
Figures: 137 x 79 x 69 cm; Infinity cove: Painted
medium-ply board
Dimensions variable

The Original Sinners, 2000
Replica fruits and berries, bark and moss, plastic
ornamental bowls, fishing wire, cooking oil, electric
pump mechanism, metal, medium-density fiberboard,
and light projector
200 x 60 x 60 cm

I (Heart) YOU (I LOVE YOU), 2000, 2000
298 colored UFO reflector caps, lamps, and holders,
Foamex, spray paint, and electronic light sequencer
(12 x 3-channel spell, fill & shimmer effect)
180 x 160 x 8 cm
Edition of 3/3 + 2 AP + 1 AC

YE$, 2001
335 ice-white Turbo reflector caps, lamps, holders, and
daisy washers, lacquered brass, enameled paint, and
electronic light sequencer (3-channel shimmer effect)
148 x 292 x 25 cm
Edition of 2/3 + 2 AP

Let's Fuck, 2001
Neon, Perspex, and transformer
10.5 x 60 x 36 cm
Edition of 5/5 + 2 AP

I Love Sex, 2002
Neon
45 x 59 x 5 cm
Edition of 1/10 + 2 AP

Black Magic Paintings Series, 2002
Boxed set of thirteen lithographs with spot varnish, print-
ed on 310 gsm tub-sized Somerset stock, box covered in
black cloth with "Black Magic" debossed on lid
Prints: various dimensions; box: 79 x 66.5 x 3 cm
Edition of 6/50 + 10 AP

Lithographs: *Black Magic, Happy Meal, Sue By Tim, Tool
Kit, Tim By Sue, Matchstick House, Blue Anchor, Belly-But-
ton Whirlpool, Chocolate Drop, Keys in a Basket, Flowers,
Stranger, Do As Thou Wilt*

Puny Undernourished Kid & Girlfriend From Hell (diptych),
2004
82 multicolored neon sections and transformers
Kid: 284 x 180 x 4 cm; Girlfriend: 280 x 210 x 4 cm
Edition of 1/3 + 2 AP

HE/SHE (diptych), 2004
Welded metal and two light projectors
HE: 185 x 148 x 96 cm; SHE: 144 x 186 x 100 cm

Untitled (Spinning Heads), 2005
Painted bronze
Tim (black): 38 x 34 x 34 cm; Sue (white): 38 x 35 x 35 cm;
plinths: 101.5 x 30.5 x 30.5 cm, inclusive 5 mm shadow gap
Edition of 1/6 + 2 AP

The Joy of Sex, 2005
Boxed set of forty lithographs printed on 300 gsm
Somerset Satin White stock, leather box portfolio
with gold embossed lettering
Prints: 42 x 29.7 cm; portfolio: 45.5 x 33 x 6 cm
Edition of 1/25 + 5 AP + 1 HC

Lithographs: *Kiss, Pretty to the Point, Hands down Pants,
Juicy Peaches, No Bra, Back to the Front, Joy Stick, 1-2-3-
4, Mouth Fuck, Violent Bliss, Easy Tiger, Phone Sex, Simply
Natural, Mind Fuck, Sweet Harmony, Pure Trouble, Lucky
Dip, Into the Groove, The Glory Hole, Suck, Selfish Cunt,
Wank, Fuck, Enter the Dragon, Chocolate Dip,
Reverse Perverse, Twin Peaks, Buttfuck, The X Factor,
Buttfuck II, Corkscrew, The 69 Club, Pumping, The Safer
Sex, Horseplay, Girlplay, Nipple Reaction, Wildlife, Fast
Fuck, Still Horny*

Black Narcissus, 2006
Black polysulfide rubber, wood, and light projector
Sculpture: 60 x 72 x 38 cm; plinth: 91.5 x 30.5 x 30.5 cm;
151.5 x 72 x 38 cm overall

fuckingbeautiful (hot pink version, detail), 2008
Three neon sections and transformers
46 x 116 x 6.5 cm
Edition of 10 + 2/2 AP + 1 HC

ARTIST BIO

Tim Noble was born in Stroud, Gloucestershire, in 1966;
Sue Webster was born in Leicester in 1967. They met
while studying fine art at Nottingham Polytechnic (now
Nottingham Trent University) in 1986, and have been
making art together for over two decades, develop-
ing their signature imagery—assemblages of personal
items and household trash—in the mid-1990s. In their
first shadow sculpture, *Miss Understood & Mr Meanor*
(1997), a light pointed at two assemblages of trash
projects a shadow portrait of the artists on the wall
behind. Parallel to the shadow sculptures are Noble
and Webster's light sculptures that reference iconic
pop culture symbols and, with the aid of complex light
sequencing, perpetually flash messages of everlasting
love (and hate). These sculptural artworks challenge
the eye by fusing opposites, creating art out of what
consumer culture has discarded and imbuing high-art
strategies with punk attitude.

Noble and Webster's solo exhibitions include
Masters of the Universe at the DESTE Foundation for
Contemporary Art, Athens (2000); *Tim Noble and
Sue Webster* at MoMA PS1, New York (2003); and
Polymorphous Perverse at the Freud Museum, London
(2006). Their work has been included in major group
exhibitions, including *Apocalypse: Beauty and Horror in
Contemporary Art* at the Royal Academy, London (2000);
Monument to Now (2005) and *Fractured Figure* (2008)
at the DESTE Foundation; *Dream & Trauma* at Kunsthalle
Wien and MUMOK, Vienna (2007); and *Skin Fruit* at the
New Museum, New York (2010). In 2011 Rizzoli published
British Rubbish, a survey of the artists' work from 1996
to 2010, with an essay by Jeffrey Deitch and texts by
Michael Bracewell and Nick Cave. Noble and Webster live
and work in London.

AUTHOR BIO

Linda Yablonsky is an art critic, author, and journalist. She was senior US art critic for Bloomberg News for five years and is a frequent contributor to *Art News*, the *Art Newspaper*, *Elle*, *Time Out New York*, *W*, *Wallpaper*, and the *New York Times's T Magazine*, among others. She is the author of numerous critical essays for exhibition catalogues and in 2001 was a founding producer of WPS1, a pioneering Internet art radio station, for MoMA PS1. From 1991 to 1999 she was creative director and host of the NightLight Readings series at Manhattan's Performing Garage. In 2012 she served as art consultant for Nicholas Jarecki's film *Arbitrage*, starring Richard Gere, Susan Sarandon, and Tim Roth. In 2015, Open Road will publish an electronic edition of *The Story of Junk* (Farrar, Straus and Giroux, 1997), her novel about drug dealing and addiction in New York's Lower East Side in the early 1980s. Yablonsky lives and works in New York.

When I met Tim Noble and Sue Webster, they were living in a two-story house in East London; we had to go upstairs to their bedroom to talk, because the whole downstairs space was filled with trash. As it happens, the first work of theirs I saw was *Dirty White Trash (with Gulls)*. My thanks to Tim and Sue for their sexy, uncompromising work, and to Linda Yablonsky for her compelling take on the Noble and Webster story so far. My thanks also to Massimiliano Gioni for his ongoing commitment to the *2000 Words* series, to Karen Marta for continuing to champion the books, and to Brendan Dugan for his inspired design concept for the series and superlative work on this particular volume.

—Dakis Joannou

Tim Noble and Sue Webster
2000 Words

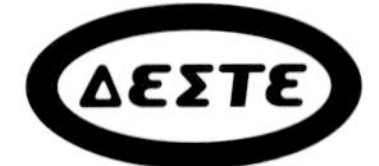

Commissioning Editor: Massimiliano Gioni
Editor: Karen Marta
Design: An Art Service
Editorial Manager: Dustin Cosentino
Coordinator: Regina Alivisatos
Registrar: Natasha Polymeropoulos
Copy Editor: Miles Champion
Production: The Production Department

Published by:
The DESTE Foundation for Contemporary Art
Filellinon 11 & Em. Pappa St.
N. Ionia 142 34, Athens
www.deste.gr

Cover: Tim Noble and Sue Webster, *Masters of the Universe*, 2000
Thank you to Andrew MacLachlan at Tim Noble and Sue Webster Studio

Distributed in the Americas by:
ARTBOOK | D.A.P.
155 Sixth Avenue, 2nd Floor
New York, NY 10013
www.artbook.com

Distributed in Europe by:
Buchhandlung Walther König
Ehrenstrasse 4
50672 Köln
www.buchhandlung-walther-koenig.de

Printed in Greece by ALTA GRAFICO S.A.

ISBN: 978-618-5039-13-4

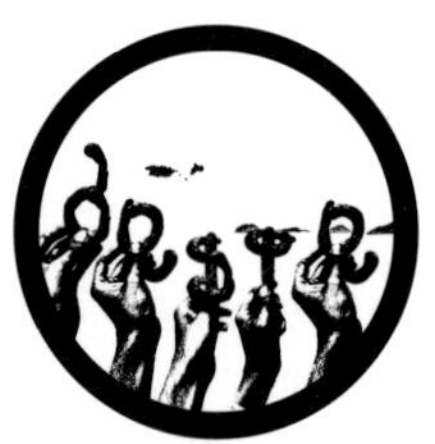